Behavioral Economics for Cost-Benefit Analysis

How should policy analysts assess "benefit validity" when behavioral anomalies appear relevant? David L. Weimer provides thoughtful answers through practical guidelines. Behavioral economists have identified a number of situations in which people appear not to behave according to the neoclassical assumptions underpinning welfare economics and its application to the assessment of the efficiency of proposed public policies through cost-benefit analysis. This book introduces the concept of benefit validity as a criterion for estimating benefits from observed or stated preference studies, and provides practical guidelines to help analysts accommodate behavioral findings. It considers benefit validity in four areas: violations of expected utility theory, unexpectedly large differences between willingness to pay and willingness to accept, non-exponential discounting, and harmful addiction. In addition to its immediate value to practicing policy analysts, it helps behavioral economists identify issues where their research programs can make practical contributions to better policy analysis.

David L. Weimer is the Edwin E. Witte Professor of Political Economy at the University of Wisconsin–Madison. He is the author of numerous articles and monographs on health policy and policy craft, as well as the co-author of two texts that have made important contributions to public policy education: *Policy Analysis: Concepts and Practice* (6th edition) and *Cost-Benefit Analysis: Concepts and Practice* (4th edition). A Fellow of the National Academy of Public Administration, he served as president of the Association for Public Policy Analysis and Management in 2006 and president of the Society for Benefit-Cost Analysis in 2013.

D1566147

Behavioral Economics for Cost-Benefit Analysis

Benefit Validity When Sovereign Consumers Seem to Make Mistakes

DAVID L. WEIMER

University of Wisconsin–Madison

CAMBRIDGE
UNIVERSITY PRESS

CAMBRIDGE
UNIVERSITY PRESS

University Printing House, Cambridge CB2 8BS, United Kingdom

One Liberty Plaza, 20th Floor, New York, NY 10006, USA

477 Williamstown Road, Port Melbourne, VIC 3207, Australia

4843/24, 2nd Floor, Ansari Road, Daryaganj, Delhi – 110002, India

79 Anson Road, #06–04/06, Singapore 079906

Cambridge University Press is part of the University of Cambridge.

It furthers the University's mission by disseminating knowledge in the pursuit of education, learning, and research at the highest international levels of excellence.

www.cambridge.org
Information on this title: www.cambridge.org/9781107197350
DOI: 10.1017/9781108178389

© David L. Weimer 2017

First published 2017

Printed in the United States of America by Sheridan Books, Inc.

A catalogue record for this publication is available from the British Library.

ISBN 978-1-107-19735-0 Hardback
ISBN 978-1-316-64766-0 Paperback

Contents

Figures

Tables

Preface

Although my graduate training in public policy exposed me to critiques of the strong rationality assumption of neoclassical economics, I did not see these critiques as posing fundamental challenges to the use of economic theory as a basis for predicting the impacts of public policies and assessing the implications of these impacts for the efficient use of society's scarce resources. Teaching risk and insurance in the 1970s certainly required me to acknowledge the limitations of the expected utility hypothesis apparent from the important work of Daniel Kahneman and Amos Tversky. However, it was not until the following decade that the relevance of behavioral findings for policy analysis became apparent to me in the course of writing a text on policy analysis with Aidan Vining: social problems that could not be satisfactorily framed using the traditionally recognized market failures required us to have a chapter on what we called "other limitations" of the competitive framework that drew on the early findings of behavioral economics. I became very aware of the importance of behavioral research for contingent valuation, an important stated pre-ference tool for valuing benefits, through my fortunate collaboration with Robert Berrens, Alok Bohara, Hank Jenkins-Smith, and Carol Silva. I began to consider the implications of behavioral economics for cost-benefit analysis more generally in a project that Aidan and I did for the MacArthur Foundation on measuring the benefits of social policies. We were particularly intrigued by addiction, a topic I address in this book along with what I see as the other most relevant behavioral chal-lenges to conventional cost-benefit analysis: failure of the expected utility hypotheses, dependence of valuations on reference points, and time inconsistency.

Welfare economics provides the conceptual foundations for cost-benefit analysis. Ideally, one would want to integrate behavioral findings into welfare economics to guide the measurement of costs and benefits. Considerable progress has been made along these lines by B. Douglas Bernheim and Antonio Rangel. However, the gap between behavioral welfare economics and the craft of cost-benefit analysis remains large—indeed, even within the long-established neoclassical framework, simple and elegant theory provides largely general guidance for those who actually do cost-benefit analysis in a complicated world with imperfect information. My primary objective in this book is to help these analysts better accommodate relevant behavioral findings within their cost-benefit analyses by providing practical guidelines for doing so. My secondary objective is to alert behavioral economists to research questions whose answers could inform better guidelines in the future.

The University of Hong Kong provided me with a sabbatical home that made writing this book not only possible but also enjoyable. I especially thank Dean John Burns and the Faculty of Social Sciences for welcoming me to the University of Hong Kong and for involving me in activities enough to make me feel like a colleague but not so much as to interfere with my research and writing. Some of the research for this project was supported by the Daniel Louis and Genevieve Rustvold Goldy Fellowship awarded by the Robert M. La Follette School of Public Affairs. I was particularly fortunate to receive encouragement, comments, or other assistance from a number of scholars: Dan Acland, Glenn Blomquist, David Greenberg, James Hammitt, Robert Haveman, Hank Jenkins-Smith, Jack Knetsch, Melanie Manion, Jonathan Renchon, Lisa Robinson, Carol Silva, Ian Thynne, Aidan Vining, W. Kip Viscusi, and two anonymous reviewers. Although they all contributed to this being a better book, I bear full responsibility for any errors and all interpretations. My thanks also to Jordan Krieger, who ably assembled the index and helped me tie up loose ends. Finally, I am grateful to Robert Dreesen of Cambridge University Press for expeditiously securing very helpful reviews that enabled me to improve the original manuscript substantially.

I

Introduction

Good policy analysis considers all relevant social goals in assessing and comparing policy alternatives. Although economic efficiency, informally meaning maximizing the value of goods produced by available resources, is rarely the only goal of public policy, it almost always is, or should be, one of the relevant goals. Cost-benefit analysis (CBA) is a protocol for systematically assessing the economic efficiency of alternatives to current policy. It provides principles and conventions for monetizing the benefits and the costs of proposed policies relative to current policy for society as a whole. Its prediction of net benefits, the difference between benefits and costs, serves as a metric for economic efficiency.

The principle of "consumer sovereignty" has been fundamental to the valuation protocols that implement the principles of what can be called neoclassical CBA. It assumes that consumers obtain utility from their consumption of goods and that they are instrumentally rational in choosing the bundles of goods that maximize their utilities subject to the income and other constraints that they face. Within this paradigm, consumers' choices reveal their valuations of goods, and these valuations can be appropriately used to monetize policy changes through their impacts on consumption of these goods. Until the 1970s, only observed consumer behaviors were the basis for inferring monetary values (so-called revealed preference methods); subsequently, survey responses to hypothetical changes have become increasingly used as the basis for inferring these values for goods for which consumption leaves insufficient behavioral traces for observational inference (so-called stated preference methods). Although some economists still question the empirical validity of stated preference methods, like revealed preferences, stated preference methods take consumer valuations at face value. That is, these methods assume that consumers know and act upon their own preferences to maximize the utilities they obtain from using their own resources, and that these preferences can be elicited through hypothetical choices posed in surveys.

Yet, empirical evidence suggests that people not only sometimes fail to act as if they are maximizing utility as assumed within the neoclassical paradigm, but that these deviations tend to be systematic and therefore predictable. People sometimes assess risky alternatives in ways that do not appear to maximize expected utility. They sometimes value tradeoffs between current and future consumption that are inconsistent with exponential time discounting to maximize the present value of utility. They sometimes value alternative bundles of consumption in terms of their initial endowments of goods rather than having utilities that depend only on actual consumption. They sometimes consume addictive goods that family and friends, or they themselves retrospectively or even prospectively, view as undesirable. They sometimes make choices that do not anticipate what will actually make them happy because of their limited imaginations about the future. Behavioral economics attempts to explain such deviations from the predicted behaviors of the neoclassical paradigm by "increasing the realism of the psychological underpinnings" in modeling the way people actually make choices (Camerer and Loewenstein 2004, 3).

Should the findings of behavioral economics be accommodated in CBA practice? If so, when and how should they be accommodated? Can the accommodations be sufficiently well grounded in economic theory to become unambiguous and credible components of valuation procedures? Can the accommodations be implemented with the types of data that can be reasonably gathered? These are the questions that this book seeks to answer.

BEHAVIORAL LANDSCAPE

In view of the numerous anomalies from the perspective of the neoclassical model of choice identified by behavioral economists, it truly seems "like a jungle out there." The appearance of anomalies potentially relevant to economic behavior should not be surprising because humans are complex and interact with their environments in complicated ways, as research in cognitive and social psychology attest. Often anomalies can be reasonably ignored, either because they only modestly affect individual choices or because the institutions within which choices are made tend to mitigate

TABLE 1.1 *Behavioral Anomalies from the Perspective of Neoclassical CBA*

General Category	Examples	CBA Relevance
Forecasting Errors	Heuristic biases Overconfidence Cognitive burdens Imagination failure Affective forecasting errors	Complicate inference
Ancillary Decision Factors	Framing effects Mode effects Incidental emotions Cues	Complicate inference Introduce additional uncertainty in valuation
Unconventional Preferences	Endowment effects Ambiguity aversion Time inconsistency Present bias Positional goods Addiction	Complicate inference Pose fundamental challenges to valuation

their impacts in aggregate or over time. However, in some cases they pose fundamental challenges to the neoclassical foundations of CBA. Before addressing specific anomalies in subsequent chapters, an overview of the behavioral landscape provides some useful context.

For the purpose at hand, a division of anomalies into three general categories in the leftmost column of Table 1.1 provides a rough map. The first category, forecasting errors, includes cases in which individuals are assumed to have well-formulated preferences but do not process available information adequately to make decisions that maximize the value of their consumption in terms of their own preferences. The classification of biases resulting from heuristics commonly used by people facing risk is one of the seminal contributions to behavioral economics (Tversky and Kahneman 1974). Research suggests that people have a "pervasive tendency" toward overconfidence (Chambers and Windschitl 2004, 813). People often have difficulty assessing complicated information, especially when facing more than a modest number of alternative choices (Miller 1956). People may also fail to imagine the full range of choices or possible outcomes (Le Grand and New 2015; Acland 2015) or accurately forecast the feelings that the outcomes will produce (Wilson and Gilbert 2003).

Such forecasting errors do not necessarily challenge either the usefulness of neoclassical utility as a construct or the assumption that individuals make decisions to maximize it. One can imagine providing people with sufficient information, coaching, and time to allow them to forecast without bias so that they would make decisions consistent with utility maximization such that their preferences would be revealed and could be used as a basis for valuation in CBA. However, in the presence of biases, neither actual nor hypothetical decisions directly reveal preferences, so inference about them is complicated.

The second category, the dependence of decisions on ancillary factors, recognizes that the circumstances of choice can affect the choices made. The term "ancillary" identifies factors that affect decisions but are not relevant to the value of the resulting consumption to the individual. The way choice situations are framed often introduces ancillary factors (Kahneman and Tversky 1984). Eliciting choices with different modes, such as choices of lotteries versus stated values (Lichtenstein and Slovic 1971), can result in inconsistent choices. Emotions not directly related to the decision at hand can nonetheless affect the choices individuals make (Loewenstein and Lerner 2003). Environmental cues, perhaps arousing emotions, can affect choices as well (Laibson 2001; Bernheim and Rangel 2004).

Like forecasting errors, ancillary decision factors complicate inference about preferences. Because the identification of all relevant ancillary factors may be impractical, especially in observational studies, it may not be possible to isolate preferences relevant to the value of consumption. Consequently, the presence of ancillary factors may make valuation more uncertain than if they were not present.

The third category, unconventional preferences, refers to valuations of consumption by individuals that are inconsistent with standard neoclassical assumptions. Instead of valuing the quantities of goods consumed, consumers sometimes make decisions as if they were valuing decisions in terms of changes in quantities of goods relative to some initial endowment (Kahneman et al. 1990). Consumers may also make choices under uncertainty that seem to display an irrational aversion to ambiguity (Ellsberg 1961) or decisions over time that appear inconsistent with stable underlying preferences (Laibson 1997). Costly self-control in the face of temptations may result in a present bias in which consumers make decisions that they regret (O'Donoghue and Rabin 2015). In some circumstances preferences appear to depend not just on consumption but also on one's consumption position relative to some reference group (Carlsson et al. 2007). Although some features of addiction can be captured within the neoclassical framework (Becker and Murphy 1988), I nonetheless include addictive consumption as an example of unconventional preferences because the models of rational addiction do not appear to capture fully the extreme present bias addiction sometimes induces. All of these examples pose challenges to the routine ways policy impacts are valued in CBA.

I purposely exclude from this list two types of preferences sometimes viewed as anomalous to the neoclassical framework. First, people may place a value on consumption by others. Such other-regarding preferences can be directly accommodated within the neoclassical framework by allowing individuals' utilities to depend not just on the goods they consume but on some goods consumed by others. The existence of such altruistic preferences can complicate inference but does not pose a fundamental challenge to valuation. Second, people may place a value on the way collective decisions are made. As with other-regarding preferences, these process-regarding preferences can be captured in individuals' utilities like other public goods. Again, their presence complicates inference about preferences but does not fundamentally challenge preferences as the basis for valuation.

A few of the examples in Table 1.1, specifically imagination failure, incidental emotions, and positional goods, are not addressed in this investigation of the implications of behavioral economics for CBA. Several others, particularly heuristic biases, endowment effects, time inconsistency, present bias, and addiction, receive most of the attention because they are frequently encountered, pose particularly serious challenges, or both.

GENERAL APPROACH

Concerns about the implications of behavioral economics for CBA have elicited three types of intellectual responses: First, some scholars see revealed or stated preferences as an inappropriate basis for assessing the relative efficiency of alternative public policies, especially in the context of the many behavioral challenges to the neoclassical paradigm. Such responses are often based on one of two misconceptions about CBA as a tool of policy analysis. The first misconception confuses efficiency with wellbeing. For example, Bronsteen and colleagues (2013) suggest replacing CBA with wellbeing analysis based on surveys of people's stated assessments of their own subjective wellbeing, or happiness. The numerous practical difficulties aside, this sort of wellbeing analysis fails to appreciate that the purpose of CBA is to inform public policy decisions about the efficient use of resources. Maximizing efficiency in the use of resources does not necessarily maximize happiness, as the latter depends on more than the consumption of goods. The second misconception is to treat CBA as if it were a decision rule. For example, Brennan (2014) suggests abandoning CBA in favor of greater reliance on democratic delegation of authority to make regulations. However, one would be hard pressed to find any significant case of policy making in representative government in which CBA is a decisive decision rule rather than an input to the policy making process. Indeed, a case can be made that CBA has too little influence compared to organized and concentrated interests in representative governments (Vining and Weimer 1992). I reject both these fundamental challenges to CBA.

A second type of intellectual response has been attempts to revise welfare economics, the conceptual foundation of CBA, so that it does not depend on assumptions that behavioral economics research finds often violated. For example, Sugden (2004), Bernheim and Rangel (2007), and Bernheim (2016) provide conceptually coherent behavioral alternatives to neoclassical welfare economics. Most such attempts represent an intellectually attractive broadening of perspective in which neoclassical welfare economics emerges as the special case in the absence of behavioral anomalies. Unfortunately, these frameworks do not directly inform the practice of CBA—one might make the same objection to the welfare theorems based on the general equilibrium model of the idealized competitive economy that provides the conceptual underpinning for neoclassical CBA. Nonetheless, like the neoclassical welfare theorems, these efforts to construct a behavioral welfare theory provide intellectual resources potentially useful in developing practical guidance and therefore, I believe, deserve more attention.

A third intellectual response involves accommodating behavioral challenges within the existing CBA framework on a case-by-case basis. It means identifying the relevant behavioral challenges in particular contexts, assessing their likely importance for both the prediction and valuation of policy impacts, and adapting standard methods to accommodate them in a consistent and transparent way when they are important. I see this as the general approach taken by Robinson and Hammitt (2011) in their review of behavioral implications for CBA conducted for the Society for Benefit-Cost Analysis. I do not view the case-by-case approach pejoratively, as might someone seeking a simple general response to behavioral challenges. Rather, as the goal of this book is the development of useful guidance for those actually doing CBA, I embrace it.

MORE THAN JUST AN INTELLECTUAL EXERCISE

CBA has a long history of use by the US federal government. Its origin appears to have been an effort by Congress to shift infrastructure investments toward the commonweal by demanding some justification for what was going into the pork barrel. As early as the River and Harbor Act of 1902, the Army Corps of Engineers, the designer and builder of water resource projects like canals, dams, and harbors, was required to quantify costs and benefits, but the first explicit requirement for CBA appeared in the River and Harbor Act of 1920 (Hammond 1966). The modern era of CBA began with the Flood Control Act of 1936, the guidelines complied by the Federal Interagency River Basin Committee, or so-called Green Book, and the subsequent compilation of CBA guidelines in the Bureau of the Budget Circular A-47 in 1952 (Hanley and Spash 1993).

Executive orders requiring federal cabinet departments to conduct CBAs of major proposed rules and their alternatives greatly expanded its use. President Nixon directed federal agencies to specify regulatory alternatives and their costs (Copeland 2011), and President Ford required agencies to prepare inflation impact statements for proposed rules (Executive Order 11821). President Carter took a step toward CBA by requiring agencies to consider the cost-effectiveness of alternative rules (Executive Order 12044). The framework for contemporary requirements for the use of CBA in the rulemaking process, the Regulatory Impact Analysis (RIA), was introduced by President Reagan in 1981 (Executive Order 12291). It applied to rules agencies proposed that would have an annual effect on the economy of $100 million or more in terms of costs, benefits, or transfers, and directed agencies to choose alternative rules that offered the largest net benefits. The Office of Management and Budget assumed an oversight role in the RIA process. President Clinton expanded the set of rules for which RIAs must be conducted and created the Office of Information and Regulatory Affairs in the Office of Management and Budget to take the lead oversight role (Executive Order 12866). President Obama reaffirmed the major provisions of the Clinton order (Executive Order 13563). He also strengthened provisions in the Reagan and Clinton executive orders requiring agencies to conduct retrospective analyses to assess the accuracy of predicted costs and benefits of major rules analyzed in prior RIAs to determine if continuation of existing rules was economically justified (Lutter 2013). He subsequently required agencies to submit their review plans to the Office of Management and Budget (Executive Order 13610) and urged independent agencies (those with commissioners appointed for fixed terms and not subject to executive order) to adopt voluntarily the RIA requirements imposed on cabinet departments (Executive Order 13579).

To help analysts conduct RIAs, the Office of Management and Budget has issued a series of guidelines for doing CBA. Most recently, it worked with the Council of Economic Advisors to update the guidelines substantially in Circular A-4 (OMB 2003). A number of agencies, most notably the Environmental Protection Agency (US EPA 2014), have issued their own supplemental guidelines. Congress has put the CBA requirements found in RIAs into statute in a number of cases (Morrison 1998). Further, Congress ordered agencies proposing regulations that require significant expenditures by state, local, or tribal governments to be subjected to CBA through the Unfunded Mandates Act (PL 104–4), and it required the CBAs in RIAs to be filed with the Government Accountability Office through the so-called Congressional Review Act (PL 104–121).

The number of RIAs conducted each year is large. The Office of Management and Budget estimates that over the ten-year period from fiscal year 2005 through fiscal year 2014, almost 3,000 of the more than 36,000 final rules issued by federal agencies were subjected to its review under Executive Orders 12866 and 13563 (US OMB 2015, 7).

It summarized predicted costs and benefits for the 120 of the 549 major rules it reviewed that met the major rule criteria through annual costs or benefits (rather than just transfers) and were supported by RIAs with substantial monetization done either by the agency or its staff: in 2010 dollars, aggregate annual benefits were between $260.9 billion and $981.0 billion, and aggregate annual costs were between $68.4 billion and $102.9 billion (US OMB 2015, 10). These magnitudes show the importance of rulemaking to the economy, and therefore the potential impact of CBA in improving economic efficiency through the RIA process. Unfortunately, we have little empirical evidence about the realization of this potential (Hahn and Tetlock 2008; Shapiro and Morrall 2012). Nonetheless, it is likely that the expectation of having to produce plausible CBAs of proposed rules deters agencies from advocating very inefficient rules and promotes consideration of efficiency-enhancing modifications during rule development.

Behavioral economics has substantial relevance in a number of regulatory areas, both in terms of identifying market failures (the ways that choices made by individual market participants fail to maximize efficiency overall) and in applying CBA to assess the relative efficiency of alternative rules. In 2015 President Obama directed agencies to consider behavioral insights in their policy designs (Executive Order 13707). A cross-agency working group, the Social and Behavioral Science Team, was created to support implementation of the order. It is currently focusing on eight policy areas: "promoting retirement security, advancing economic opportunity, improving college access and affordability, responding to climate change, supporting criminal justice reform, assisting job seekers, helping families get health coverage and stay healthy, and improving the effectiveness and efficiency of Federal Government operations" (US Social and Behavioral Sciences Team 2016, viii).

One regulatory area in which behavioral economics has a potentially important role is consumer finance, the domain of the relatively new Consumer Financial Protection Bureau (CFPB). Along with classic market failures such as externalities and informational asymmetries, financial regulation can potentially increase economic efficiency by mitigating behavioral biases and cognitive limitations of consumers (Campbell et al. 2011). However, the Government Accountability Office found that the CFPB and other financial regulators face both conceptual and empirical challenges in confidently applying CBA to consumer financial protection rules (US GAO 2014).

More generally, behavioral economics suggests ways that public policies can nudge individuals toward possibly better choices through manipulation of the "architecture of choice" (Thaler and Sunstein 2008). Changing defaults, forcing decisions, or encouraging better decisions by simplifying choices are behavioral-based policy interventions (Madrian 2014; Bhargava and Loewenstein 2015). For example, requiring potential program participants to opt-out rather than opt-in can be used to nudge participation in activities such as saving, organ donation, and vaccination that are generally viewed as socially desirable. When the desirability of participation is specific to individuals, forcing an active decision rather than relying on defaults may improve decisions. Individuals may make better decisions if their task is simplified through reductions in the number of options, standardization of options, or the provision of individualized information.

The proper way to assess the benefits of these sorts of nudges in CBA is not always clear—a challenge for analysts that will increase as their use and the use of other behaviorally-based policies become more common (Oliver 2013). It also prompts revisiting of the role of paternalism in public policy. Thaler and Sunstein (2003) classify nudges as consistent with what they call "libertarian paternalism," a form of paternalism that they argue does not violate individual autonomy. The underlying argument is that nudges affect individuals' choice processes, or means, but not their ends. Le Grand and New (2015) seek to identify the normative rationale for paternalistic public policies such as nudges. They define governmental interventions as paternalistic if they are intended to "(a) address a failure of judgment by that individual and (b) to further the individual's own good" (p. 2), and propose that the failure of judgment, or means, be determined by empirical evidence, while the individual's own good, or ends, be those stated by the individual. Acland (2015) notes that some of the same behavioral research about people's ability to imagine their futures also applies to ends, so that furthering the individual's own good could also justify government paternalism within the Le Grand and New framework. In any event, the justification for a nudge relies on an assessment that a change in the circumstances of choice will increase the benefits that accrue to the choosers.

A proposed rulemaking by the Food and Drug Administration (FDA) regarding tobacco regulation illustrates the sort of controversy that behavioral issues can raise with respect to the assessment of benefits. In 2009 Congress gave the FDA authority to regulate tobacco products through the Family Smoking Prevention and Tobacco Control Act (PL 111–31). In 2010 the FDA proposed a rule that would make health warnings about cigarette smoking more graphic in labeling and advertising, like the pictorial warnings used in Canada (US FDA 2010). Its CBA recognized that consumers obtain pleasure from smoking, monetized in neoclassical analysis as consumer surplus, the value of the quantity consumed in excess of the amount paid for that quantity. To take account of lost consumer surplus, the analysts reduced estimates of the morbidity and mortality benefits by half (p. 69544). This arbitrary approach drew criticism from health analysts, who rejected the general neoclassical approach to addiction and this particular ad hoc adjustment to take account of consumer loss (Chaloupka et al. 2015). Subsequent efforts within the Department of Health and Human Services to develop a sound basis for taking account of losses of consumer surplus when regulations reduce consumption of harmfully addictive goods such as cigarettes was halted in the face of criticism from public health advocates (Begley and Clarke 2015).

Federal regulatory agencies are not the only government producers of CBA in the United States. High-quality and influential CBAs are routinely produced by the Washington State Institute for Public Policy (WSIPP), an organization serving its state legislature (Weimer and Vining 2009). WSIPP developed a CBA tool that is "evidence-based" in drawing on meta-analyses of the impacts of criminal justice programs as a basis for systematically assessing and comparing their costs and benefits. Its CBA was influential in the Washington legislature's decision to invest in a portfolio of programs aimed at reducing incarceration rather than building a new prison (Aos et al. 2006). Subsequently, WSIPP expanded its CBA tool to cover a number of other social policy areas. Recognizing the success of the WSIPP efforts, the MacArthur Foundation and the Pew Charitable Trusts joined forces to support states and localities in adapting the WSIPP CBA tool through the Results First Initiative (Pew-MacArthur Fact Sheet, 2015). Even prior to the Results First Initiative, 48 states had statutory mandates for the application of CBA in specific contexts (White and Van Landingham 2015).

Many important social and public health problems confronted by state and local governments raise behavioral issues. For example, people who abuse substances such as alcohol or allow themselves to become obese may impose negative effects on others, providing a neoclassical rationale for public intervention, but they may impose the greatest harm on themselves, at least from the perspective of the public health profession if not in their own view. If consumers have full information about these self-harms, then neoclassical CBA would not count their reductions as benefits.

It would be mistaken to think of CBA as only an American practice. Of the 35 members of the Organization for Economic Cooperation and Development, 32 now have requirements for RIA, many of which include CBA as a component (Deighton-Smith et al. 2016). For example, since 2007, the Cabinet Directive on Streamlining Regulation has required Canadian departments and agencies to assess both regulatory and non-regulatory policies with CBA (Canada TB 2007). The UK Treasury Department recommends CBA in its guidance for the appraisal and evaluation of projects by the central government (UK Treasury 2003, 3). The Australia Productivity Commission, which provides advice to the Australian government on microeconomic issues, conducts CBA and strongly advocates its use for large infrastructure projects (Australia PC 2015). Applications to the European Union's Cohesion Fund, which provides funding for transportation and environmental projects in the less wealthy member states, must be accompanied by CBAs (Florio 2006). Although concerns have been raised about their declining frequency and quality, CBAs are still often done as part of prospective and retrospective assessments of World Bank projects (IEG 2010).

In recent years, the notion of assessing programs implemented by NGOs through a calculation of their social rate of return on investment (SROI) has become widespread (Arvidson et al. 2013). NGOs quantify and monetize the outcomes they produce and compare them to the cost of the resources expended. To the extent that the monetization is intended to capture social value, CBA provides the proper protocols for its efficiency component. Indeed, the very term has long been used in CBA as the basis for choosing among alternative investment projects. Deviations of SROI from CBA would mainly arise if the NGO or its sponsors were valuing distributional or other impacts rather than just the efficiency impacts of its program. Not surprisingly, organizations face many of the same challenges in conducting SROIs as they would in doing CBAs (Millar and Hall 2013).

A policy instrument, the social impact bond, seeks to raise private capital for public purposes in the spirit of the SROI (Warner 2013). Governments or foundations create the opportunity for securing private sector investment in the provision of public services by promising payment to organizations for some measurable outcome. If a social impact bond is to promote some policy goal in an efficient manner, then the payments that governments or foundations promise for performance should be based not just on some single measurable outcome, but on the full range of impacts. Properly valuing these impacts again requires CBA protocols, such as those for valuing reductions in crime for criminal justice social impact bonds (Fox and Albertson 2011).

CBA protocols also have a potential role to play in the pricing of environmental services. Changing forestry, agricultural, and mining practices may produce positive externalities ranging from clean water directly valuable in production and consumption to preservation of species with public good value. For example, paying countries to preserve rain forests may contribute to the preservation of biodiversity as well as reduce net carbon emissions (Weimer 1990; Karsenty et al. 2014). Although most programs that pay for environmental services set prices to compensate for the costs of producing the services (Wunder et al. 2008), assessing the social value of the services requires the use of CBA techniques. Ultimately, the social value of the services less the cost of producing them determines whether these programs are efficient and therefore worthy candidates for replication or expansion.

Returning to the public sector, an important theme in public administration over the last two decades has been that the fundamental task of the public manager is to create public value (Moore 1995; Benington and Moore 2010). How should public value be measured? Thompson and Rizova (2015) argue for doing so with CBA. They also observe that the new public management, which seeks to make public organizations more businesslike, does not necessarily promote public value because of its focus on production, or technical, efficiency rather than social value. Clearly, public value goes beyond the efficient use of resources. Nonetheless, it is hard to imagine creating public value without at least some guidance from CBA.

As discussed, CBA has been institutionalized by a number of national governments and international organizations. At least in the United States, its use by subnational governments is increasing, along with general demands to make better use of limited resources through evidence-based policy. Whether or not fully acknowledged, it should inform innovations in the provision of public services by NGOs and public agencies. Further, the increasing application of CBA to social policies inevitably encounters issues raised by behavioral economics. Consequently, the subject of this book has practical implications as well as scholarly relevance.

ROADMAP

The next two chapters provide useful background and conceptual resources. Chapter 2 reviews neoclassical welfare economics as the foundation for conventional CBA. It explains the role of CBA in policy analysis, reviews the development of valuation principles from neoclassical welfare economics, discusses the assumptions and concerns that arise in moving from valuation principles to their application in CBA, and identifies the most behaviorally contestable elements of neoclassical welfare economics. It seeks to explain not only what CBA is intended to do, namely assess the relative efficiency of policies in terms of the use of scarce resources, but what it is not intended to do, namely identify the policy that maximizes social welfare in the vernacular sense of the term. This clarification makes clear why metrics other than net social benefits should be seen as CBA alternatives rather than CBA improvements.

Behavioral economists have not ignored the welfare implications of their findings. Chapter 3 considers three prominent intellectual efforts to accommodate behavioral findings in the assessment of welfare. These approaches seek to provide guidance when consumers' choices appear irrational from the neoclassical perspective. First, the most radical approach seeks nothing less than a redefinition of welfare economics in terms of maximizing opportunity rather than preference satisfaction, a change that preserves consumer sovereignty in the face of inconsistent preferences. Although it shows that the ideal competitive economy would maximize opportunity just as the neoclassical market achieves Pareto efficiency, it does not provide a practical way to compare the relative opportunity for policies to correct the market failures that prevent the competitive economy from achieving the ideal. Second, the most comprehensive approach accommodates inconsistent preferences by breaking the link between choices and revealed preferences, allowing choice to reflect both neoclassical preferences and ancillary conditions not relevant to preference satisfaction. In addition to providing a useful conceptual framework, it provides some reassurance that small deviations from rationality will have only small impacts on neoclassical welfare assessment. Third, a less ambitious but more directly useful approach makes a distinction between decision utility, the satisfaction individuals anticipate from available alternatives, and experience utility, the satisfaction individuals actually receive from chosen alternatives. The distinction between decision and experience utility can be usefully applied in addressing a number of behavioral challenges to CBA.

The next four chapters address the four most important of these behavioral challenges. Chapter 4 considers the implications of individuals not making choices consistent with the expected utility hypothesis in circumstances involving risk. To help frame the discussion, the chapter sets out prospect theory as the most prominent behavioral alternative to the expected utility hypothesis. In prospect theory individuals employ subjective probabilities (decision weights) rather than evidence-based probabilities in comparing risky alternatives, a deviation from expected utility that accommodates the substantial body of evidence supporting the generalization that individuals have difficulty estimating and using probabilities. Deviations between subjective and evidence-based probabilities raise a number of concerns, especially in the context of using evidence from existing research to inform valuations in CBA in what is commonly called "benefit transfer." Assessing these sources of information requires not only consideration of internal and external validity, but also the assessment of what the chapter defines as "benefit validity": the appropriateness of interpreting benefits (which may be positive or negative) based on the assumption that individuals act rationality when they may actually be acting otherwise. Benefit validity allows application of what Viscusi and Gayer (2016) call the "behavioral transfer test." Market processes may preserve benefit validity in revealed preference studies despite individual irrationality. Stated preference studies require explicit efforts to communicate risk effectively to increase benefit validity.

Chapter 5 addresses the longstanding controversy surrounding the often large gap between willingness to pay and willingness to accept as measures of benefits. The gap was once widely viewed as consistent with the behavioral model of individual valuation of gains and losses from a reference point but not with neoclassical axioms. However, even within the neoclassical paradigm a large gap is possible if the public good being valued does not have close substitutes among available private goods. Both the behavioral and neoclassical paradigms bring into question the common practice of framing stated preference elicitations in terms of willingness to pay even when the reality of the policy change calls for willingness to accept. However, there remain a number of practical difficulties in implementing willingness-to-accept elicitations related to incentive incompatibility, especially the absence of an individual budget constraint.

Chapter 6 considers the implications of behavioral research showing that people often make intertemporal choices that show short-run impatience inconsistent with the exponential time discounting universally employed in the application of CBA to policies with intragenerational impacts. Strong arguments can be made for the continued use of exponential discounting of future costs and benefits to assess the efficiencies of alternative policies in terms of their present values even when individuals make immediate choices inconsistent with exponential discounting. However, the implications of non-exponential discounting for benefit validity are less clear. The most promising framing involves focusing on immediate temptations and the disutility of the self-control needed to resist them. Willingness to pay for reductions in the costs of self-control, such as through limiting exposure to temptations, is a conceptually attractive basis for predicting benefits, but finding ways to measure this willingness to pay poses a substantial challenge to integrating behavioral findings about impatience into CBA.

Harmful addictive consumption and habits strongly challenge the neoclassical paradigm. Chapter 7 begins with a review of efforts to construct neoclassical models in which consumers rationally engage in addictive consumption. Behavioral economics provides several explanations for the occurrence of addiction, including misperception of risks, non-exponential discounting, response to cues, and costly self-control against temptation, that involve less than fully rational choices. Using these explanations to guide benefit valuation, however, is not straightforward. Most importantly, although some harmful goods often become addictive once someone starts consuming them, whether they actually become addictive depends on the particular individual as well. The great heterogeneity among individuals with respect to their propensity for addiction greatly complicates moving from market data to benefit estimation. For some legally available goods, it may be useful to sever the relationship between demand and marginal valuation schedules by distinguishing between market demand and unaddicted consumption.

Chapters 2 through 7 propose practical guidelines (PGLs) for doing CBA. Chapter 8 collects these guidelines together and reviews them in terms of their bases in theory and evidence. As with any scholarly endeavor, I hope that the process of developing these guidelines is informative to readers. However, I intend the guidelines themselves to be useful to CBA practitioners in accommodating the findings of behavioral economics. I also hope that these explicit guidelines attract attention from researchers, especially in drawing more behavioral economists into discussions about CBA. Of course, I hope that the guidelines will enjoy support and friendly amendment, but from the perspective of helping CBA promote good public policy, challenges may be just as valuable.

2

Neoclassical Valuation Principles for CBA

Welfare economics primarily addresses the efficiency of allocations of goods within an economy. CBA employs the concepts of welfare economics to assess the relative efficiency of public policies that would alter the otherwise occurring allocation of goods. In a neoclassical world of instrumentally rational consumers with stable preferences, welfare economics provides clear principles for monetizing policy-induced changes in consumption incurred by individuals. With a few additional assumptions about the interpretation of efficiency, the aggregation of these amounts of money through algebraic summation across individuals provides a measure of the total value of the policy change to society that can be compared to the cost to society of the real resources (labor, land, capital) needed to implement it. Although not all conceptual issues have been fully resolved within neoclassical welfare economics, the greatest challenges that arise in actually doing CBA lie not in disputes over finer points of theory but rather in limitations in data and analytical resources.

This chapter presents neoclassical welfare economics from a public policy perspective and sketches its essential elements for framing discussion of the behavioral challenges it faces. As welfare economics often receives book-length treatments (e.g., Boadway and Bruce 1984; Just et al. 2004), its coverage is necessarily selective. The presentation is as nontechnical as possible to maximize accessibility.

WELFARE ECONOMICS, CBA, AND POLICY ANALYSIS

We are ultimately concerned with the use of CBA to promote good public policy. This requires consideration of how CBA narrowly, and welfare economics more broadly, relate to policy analysis. A number of common misperceptions interfere with clear assessments of CBA and lead to dubious proposals for its modification or abandonment. Most importantly, many critics of CBA treat it as if it were a decision rule rather than a protocol for assessing economic efficiency.

The very name, incorporating the word "welfare," contributes to confusion about the normative content and claims of welfare economics. In common use, welfare implies wellbeing, and promoting it seems to be an appropriately broad, or even comprehensive, goal for public policy. However, welfare in this context does not refer to a broad public policy goal, but rather to the specific goal of maximizing economic efficiency. Further, it refers to a narrow definition of efficiency, namely Pareto efficiency: an allocation is Pareto efficient if it is impossible to reallocate so as to make at least one person better off without making anyone else worse off. Consequently, although economists sometimes implicitly equate efficiency with aggregate wellbeing, doing so explicitly requires one to claim that other public policy goals intended to promote the good society are not relevant to the decision at hand.

As an illustration, consider the assessment of two alternatives to current policy, A and B, in terms of three policy goals: efficiency, equity, and public acceptability. Perhaps the policy problem is a shortage of kidneys for transplantation to people with end-stage renal disease and the alternatives involve providing payments to living donors, either to compensate for costs incurred in directing donations to relatives or friends (Alternative A) or to encourage healthy people to make undirected donations to the pool of available organs (Alternative B). Panel a in Figure 2.1 shows the simple display that would facilitate multi-goal analysis of the three policies (Weimer and Vining 2011). Unless one policy dominates the other two in terms of all the goals, the ultimate choice of a policy would require consideration of tradeoffs among the goals. For example, paying people to make undirected donations might offer the greatest efficiency but have the lowest public acceptability. However, if the only goal is efficiency, then panel b displays the information needed for a comparison. Further, as the application of welfare economics generally involves comparisons of alternative allocations, the analytical framework reduces to that shown in panel c, which assesses the efficiency of alternatives A and B relative to current policy. Finally, if sufficient data and analytical resources exist to monetize all the efficiency impacts, then CBA can be employed, as in panel d.

In this cascade, CBA becomes a decision rule only in panel d. Many CBA critics write as if CBA were commonly employed as a decision rule in

Panel a:

	Current Policy	Alternative A	Alternative B
Efficiency			
Equity			
Public Acceptability			

Panel b:

	Current Policy	Alternative A	Alternative B
Efficiency			

Panel c:

	Alternative A relative to Current Policy	Alternative B relative to Current Policy
Efficiency		

Panel d:

	Alternative A relative to Current Policy	Alternative B relative to Current Policy
Efficiency (monetized)	net benefits	net benefits

Panel e:

	Alternative A relative to Current Policy	Alternative B relative to Current Policy
Efficiency (monetized)	net benefits	net benefits
Equity		
Public acceptability		

FIGURE 2.1 Multi-Goal Policy Analysis, Welfare Economics, and CBA

this way. However, rarely is efficiency the only relevant policy goal, especially in assessing social policies, so it usually should not be the decision rule. More relevant to the critiques, it almost never is privileged as a decision rule. Indeed, one would be hard pressed to find *any* major public policy decision made by a representative government in which CBA was designated as the *sole* basis for a decision. Rather, CBA most often provides a protocol for assessing the relative efficiency of alternatives within the context of a multi-goal analysis.

Returning to Figure 2.1, panel e shows this most common application of CBA in assessing relative efficiency within a multi-goal framework. It directly reflects the description of the use of CBA in the RIA process discussed in the previous chapter. Specifically, the Office of Management and Budget's Circular A-4 calls for treating distributional impacts as a goal distinct from efficiency: "Your regulatory analysis should provide a separate description of distributional effects (i.e., how both benefits and costs are distributed among subpopulations of particular concern) so that decision makers can properly consider them along with the effects on economic efficiency" (US OMB 2003, Section D). Although in practice it appears that minimal attention is given to distributional impacts in RIAs (Robinson et al. 2016), taking account of distributional impacts in addition to CBA is nonetheless a formally recognized component of federal regulatory analysis. More generally, good analysis seeks to identify the tradeoffs among competing values to facilitate, one must hope, better political choice.

Admittedly, welfare economists have considered how values like equity or fairness could be integrated with efficiency into a single metric through a social welfare function that would provide a social ordering of alternative allocations of goods (Boadway and Bruce 1984). This project, however, faces severe challenges that make it quixotic. At the most fundamental level, Arrow (1951) showed that no social choice rule for combining individual preference orderings to produce a social preference ordering can be perfected if there are three or more alternatives. Specifically, no social choice rule can simultaneously satisfy four fairness axioms (no individual preference orderings should be excluded; no dictator should determine the social ordering; the relative ranking of any two alternatives should not be influenced by the inclusion or exclusion of a third alternative; and if everyone prefers one alternative to another, then the social ordering should also prefer it to the other) and also guarantee a transitive (if x is preferred to y and y is preferred to z then x is preferred to z) social ordering. As a consequence of Arrow's theorem, one cannot expect to discover a desirable and robust social welfare function directly from the members of society. Rather, the non-dictatorship axiom is likely to be violated by the economist or philosopher who asserts the particular social welfare function to be used. At a more practical level, the information required for implementing a social welfare function generally goes much beyond that needed for assessing efficiency. Instead of changes in the prices and aggregate quantities of goods, which typically provide a basis for estimating changes in efficiency, one must know the changes in consumption, wealth, or income for all individuals or households that would result from a policy change in order to apply a social welfare function that incorporates distributional values. Even the relatively straightforward exercise of trying to build distributional values into CBA by applying weights to changes in consumption encounters the problems of selecting weights and having sufficient information on impacts to apply them consistently (Boardman et al. 2011). So, although a universally accepted social welfare function would be attractive because it would obviate the need for multi-goal analysis, its formulation is a quest for the Holy Grail rather than a viable public policy project. A less than universally accepted social choice rule would risk submerging distributional values into an overall measure rather than forcing their explicit consideration, as in multi-goal analysis.

These considerations lead to our first simple but important practical guideline (PGL):

PGL 2.1 *CBA assesses only the relative efficiency of policies; values other than efficiency may be relevant to assessing relative social welfare.*

Although this guideline responds mainly to confusion between CBA as a protocol for assessing relative efficiency and CBA as a decision rule, it also has relevance to our objective at hand. In searching for ways to accommodate behavioral economics within CBA, we should not lose sight of the narrow focus of CBA on efficiency.

EFFICIENCY AND ITS LIMITATIONS

Pareto efficiency plays a prominent role in welfare economics. It provides a definition for efficiency that obviates the need for comparisons of the utilities of consumption of different individuals. It also has intuitive appeal in that, if an allocation is not Pareto efficient, then society is forgoing gaining something for nothing. Why not favor a Pareto improvement? That is, why not favor a reallocation that would make someone better off without making anyone else worse off? Only when no more Pareto improvements are possible is the allocation Pareto efficient and any further changes that make someone better off would have to make someone else worse off as well, providing reasonable grounds for the persons made worse off to object to these changes.

If public policies could always be crafted with appropriate compensation so as to be Pareto improvements, then these policies would provide unassailable improvements over current policy in terms of efficiency. Indeed, the most common critique of CBA—that it does not actually result in Pareto improvements—would be mute. However, a second, and more fundamental, but less discussed, concern about Pareto efficiency would remain: it privileges the status quo (Scitovsky 1941; Bromley 1990). That is, assessing the efficiency of policies depends on the initial allocation of goods. Therefore, even in a world in which all public policies were Pareto improving, one could nonetheless reasonably argue for the desirability of non-Pareto improving policies if one judged the status quo allocation as grossly inequitable.

We should also recognize that each Pareto improvement would establish a new status quo that would determine whether subsequent policies would be Pareto improving. Consequently, initial policy choices could determine which of many possible Pareto-efficient allocations would eventually be reached. This path dependence suggests another reason why, even in a world in which all adopted policies were Pareto improving, one might very well argue that society should care about goals other than economic efficiency in assessing policies.

Of course, informational demands and transaction costs generally make it impossible to construct public policies that are both Pareto improvements and universally accepted as such. Almost all public policies in the first instance produce winners and losers in the sense of changes in consumption. Even a policy that would provide a benefit to everyone, such as a regulation that would result in cleaner air, might involve net losses to some people who pay more in additional taxes for the policy than they personally receive in benefits. In these situations, how can welfare economics identify efficient policies without specifying weights for adding the changes in consumption incurred by individuals?

Providing an answer for this question preoccupied welfare economists during the 1930s (Persky 2001). The desire to make economics more scientific led to a rejection of the interpersonal comparison of utilities employed by Alfred Marshall and other classical economists in their welfare analyses. However, this in turn implied that economists would not be able to give advice as scientists about public policies that created winners as well as losers. An ingenious conceptual way around this problem was proposed by Nicholas Kaldor (1939): consider the policy efficient if it would provide a sufficient increase in the goods available so that any losers could be fully compensated. As Kaldor wrote:

In all cases, therefore, where a certain policy leads to an increase in physical productivity, and thus of aggregate real income, the economist's case for the policy is quite unaffected by the question of the comparability of individual satisfactions; since in all such cases it is possible to make everybody better off than before, or at any rate to make some people better off without making anybody worse off.   (p. 550)

John R. Hicks (1939) embraced the Kaldor proposal, along with similar work then recently done by Harold Hotelling (1938). Hick's endorsement of the Kaldor proposal led to it being commonly referred to as the Kador–Hicks criterion. Later, Hicks (1942) introduced a distinction between the income changes needed to return consumers to their original levels of utility (compensating variation) after a reallocation and the income changes needed to move consumers to the levels of utility they would have had had the reallocation occurred when it does not (equivalent variation). A distinction is sometimes made between what is called the

Kaldor compensation principle and the Hicks compensation principle. The former assesses the possibility for compensation as the algebraic sum of compensating variations; the latter as the algebraic sum of equivalent variations. However, this seems to be an ex-post construction based on a distinction made by Scitovsky (1941) in his famous article showing that the original Kaldor formulation could result in a move from allocation A to allocation B being efficient and, paradoxically, the move from B back to A also being efficient. He wrote:

> We propose, therefore, to make welfare propositions on the following principle. We must first see whether it is possible in the new situation so to redistribute income as to make everybody better off than he was in the initial situation; secondly, we must see whether starting from the initial situation it is not possible by a mere redistribution of income to reach a position superior to the new situation, again from everybody's point of view. If the first is possible and the second impossible, we shall say that the new situation is better than the old was. If the first is impossible, but the second possible, we shall say that the new situation is worse; whereas if both are possible or both are impossible, we shall refrain from making a welfare proposition. (pp. 86–87)

This test is referred to as the Kaldor–Hicks–Scitovsky criterion. It would be implemented by separately calculating the algebraic sum of both compensating variations and equivalent variations—these sums differ as a result of income effects. When income effects are small, they will be very close, as well as close to measures of welfare based on observed market demand schedules (Willig 1976), so the region of indeterminacy will also be small.

Other theoretical concerns about the Kaldor–Hicks (or the Kaldor–Hicks–Scitovsky) criterion have been raised (Boadway 1974; Mishan 1976; Blackorby and Donaldson 1990). Several of the theoretical concerns can be dismissed if a weak rather than a strong version of the compensation test is employed. The strong version assesses utilities with the resulting prices before any compensation is made; the weak version allows prices to adjust following compensation (Just et al. 2004: Appendix 9.C).

In the actual practice of CBA, the efficiency criterion is a step further from Kaldor–Hicks. The criterion for a policy to be efficient relative to current policy is for it to have positive net benefits. Benefits consist of the positive amounts people would be willing to pay (WTP) to obtain, or the amounts they would have to be paid to accept (WTA), the impacts of the policy—the latter totted as negative benefits. If willingness to pay includes all the impacts of the policy, including the use of resources needed to implement it, then net benefits would simply be the algebraic sum of these amounts. However, the willingness to pay amounts typically focus on the primary impacts of the policy and ignore reductions in goods that result from the use of resources to produce the primary impacts—reductions that one could expect to be spread widely over all members of society. These reductions in goods from the use of resources to produce a policy are captured in the opportunity cost of the resources: their values in their next best alternative uses. Net benefits are then approximated as the difference between the aggregate willingness to pay (and accept) amounts for changes in the goods directly affected by the policy minus the opportunity cost of the resources needed to implement the policy.

For example, consider a bridge that would make travel for a group of consumers more convenient. Building the bridge would require the use of labor, equipment, and materials that could be used to produce other things of value to consumers. One way to measure net benefits would require all of the consumers to anticipate how the project would change all the goods that they consume. If this were possible, then net benefits would simply be the algebraic sum of all their willingness to pay (accept) amounts. However, it is usually impractical to trace the reductions in all other goods resulting from the diversion of resources to construction of the bridge. It is likely to be more practical to impute the consumers' willingness to pay (accept) amounts for bridge access to estimate the benefit of the bridge and separately estimate the opportunity cost of the resources needed to construct it. So, for example, the willingness to pay might be estimated as the value of time savings to consumers over the expected life of the bridge, and the opportunity cost as the respective wages, rental fees, and prices for the labor, equipment, and materials needed for construction and operation. The net benefits would then be the difference between the aggregate value of time savings and the opportunity cost of construction and operation.

Whether applied through the strong compensation, the weak compensation, or the net benefits test, assessment of policies is in terms of potential Pareto efficiency. Consequently, policies assessed as efficient do not guarantee that everyone is actually made better off, only that their gains would be sufficient to make everyone better off through costless redistribution. It is this leap from Pareto efficiency to potential Pareto efficiency that motivates some of the most vigorous criticism of CBA, as well as proposals to modify it to take account of distributional consequences.

Welfare economists have recognized the significance of the leap to potential Pareto efficiency but have nonetheless offered several justifications for the use of CBA as a decision rule. One defense, advanced initially by Hicks (1941), argues that, if CBA were consistently applied, then over time it is likely that everyone would indeed be made better off. In other words, continually applying CBA to the portfolio of available policies would likely achieve Pareto efficiency for the collection of adopted policies. Another defense, raised by Hotelling (1938) for public investment projects, is that the consistent use of CBA would tend to distribute projects geographically so as to tend to produce positive net benefits for various demographic groups and regions. He also argued that, because such projects would be disproportionately funded by the very wealthy through progressive taxes, the very wealthy would be one group less likely to see positive net benefits, so CBA might actually improve the distribution of wealth in society.

As previously noted, CBA is not actually used as a decision rule anywhere, so its use in assessing efficiency within multi-goal analysis does not hinge on these sorts of defenses. However, critics of CBA sometimes argue that its monetization gives efficiency too much weight relative to the often qualitatively assessed goals in multi-goal analysis. These critiques often fail to consider the important question about the use of CBA: compared to what? Because of collective action problems, representative governments tend to be more responsive to concentrated and organized interests than to diffuse and unorganized interests (Olson 1965). In contrast, CBA assesses impacts across all members of society. For example, consider an import quota that would benefit a few domestic producers at the expense of many domestic consumers. Absent other market distortions, a competent CBA from the national perspective would find negative net benefits: the gains to the producers would be insufficient to compensate consumers for the higher prices they would pay and still make the producers better off. However, the producers who would realize large gains would be more likely to be able to coordinate collective action to influence adoption of the quota than would the much more numerous consumers who each would suffer a relatively small loss from the quota. In situations like these, use of CBA would promote not only efficiency, but also common conceptions of equity by taking account of the small losses that would otherwise be ignored in the political process (Vining and Weimer 1992). More generally, CBA can be thought of as helping to advocate for efficiency, a goal that tends not to have a very influential constituency within representative governments (Niskanen 1991).

FROM PARETO EFFICIENCY TO THE PREDICTION OF NET BENEFITS

The upper section of Figure 2.2 (up to and including 'Computable GE models') summarizes the conceptual progression from Pareto efficiency to

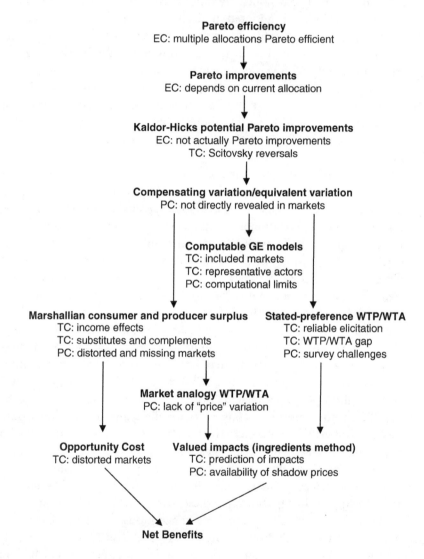

Pareto efficiency
EC: multiple allocations Pareto efficient

Pareto improvements
EC: depends on current allocation

Kaldor-Hicks potential Pareto improvements
EC: not actually Pareto improvements
TC: Scitovsky reversals

Compensating variation/equivalent variation
PC: not directly revealed in markets

Computable GE models
TC: included markets
TC: representative actors
PC: computational limits

Marshallian consumer and producer surplus
TC: income effects
TC: substitutes and complements
PC: distorted and missing markets

Stated-preference WTP/WTA
TC: reliable elicitation
TC: WTP/WTA gap
PC: survey challenges

Market analogy WTP/WTA
PC: lack of "price" variation

Opportunity Cost
TC: distorted markets

Valued impacts (ingredients method)
TC: prediction of impacts
PC: availability of shadow prices

Net Benefits

Notes: EC: ethical concern
TC: technical concern
PC: practical concern

FIGURE 2.2 Efficiency, CBA, and Concerns

compensating and equivalent variations and the concerns that arise at each step. The remainder of the figure outlines the further progression of steps to reach a prediction of net benefits.

A conceptually attractive approach is the construction of a computable general equilibrium (GE) model that allows the direct measurement of compensating and equivalent variations for changes in several related markets following a policy change (Klaiber and Smith 2012). For example, changes in school quality often have major effects on housing markets, so a comprehensive assessment of efficiency requires looking at both direct school effects and indirect housing market effects (Nechyba 2000). Similarly, linking demands in regional petroleum product markets, refining capacities, and transportation costs to well-head crude oil prices provides a basis for assessing the costs and benefits of interventions in the world oil market (Horwich et al. 1988). A regulatory example is the use of computable GE models that assess the price impacts across economic sectors to estimate the costs of air pollution regulations (US EPA 2003; see also US EPA 2015). In addition to selecting the set of markets that capture the important substitutes and complements for the primary good affected by policy, analysts must have sufficient data to link the markets together. They must also make assumptions about the utility function of consumers, often simplifying by assuming a single representative consumer. Nonetheless, computational demands are always substantial. The combinations of data limitations and the need for simplifying assumptions limit the current use of computable GE models in CBA.

The more common approach is to focus on the impact of policies on specific markets. If a policy impact changes the price or quantity in an existing market, and the market demand schedule can be estimated, then the effect of the policy on consumers can be estimated as the change in consumer surplus. However, as already noted, this change in Marshallian surplus differs from compensating and equivalent variations because of income effects. If a supply schedule can be estimated, it provides the basis for measuring changes in producer surplus—payments to suppliers in excess of the minimum amounts needed to elicit the provided supply. When markets are distorted, analysts may have to distinguish between the market demand schedule and the true marginal valuation schedule for consumers (how much they value incremental additions to consumption) to measure consumer surplus appropriately, and between the market supply schedule and the true marginal cost schedule (how much incremental additions to supply increase opportunity cost) to measure producer surplus appropriately.

A more fundamental problem often interferes with the textbook approach to valuation: missing markets. That is, often the good being produced through public policy is not traded in a market. For example, no market exists for directly estimating the benefits of noise reduction. To get around this problem, analysts often turn to the market analogy approach to estimate willingness to pay or willingness to accept. Although there is no market for buying and selling mortality risks, people do face tradeoffs between mortality risk and other things they value, such as wages or travel time. If there is sufficient variation in risks and "prices" like wage differences, then analysts can estimate how much people appear to be willing to pay to reduce their mortality risks (Viscusi and Aldy 2003). Sometimes goods (or bads) that vary by location, such as nearness to high-voltage power lines, can be valued because markets capitalize them in land prices (Sims and Dent 2005).

Some policies produce goods for which analysts cannot construct market analogies. Many environmental goods, such as the preservation of wilderness or endangered species, do not provide sufficient data from choices by consumers to allow for the application of revealed preference methods. Including them in CBA requires turning to stated preference methods, such as contingent valuation, to estimate willingness to pay for increases or willingness to accept decreases in their quantity or quality. Although some economists remain skeptical of stated preference methods (Hausman 2012), these methods are now widely accepted and employed in environmental policy (Arrow et al. 1993, Bateman and Willis 1999, Carson 2012, Freeman et al. 2014) and increasingly in other policy areas (e.g. Noonen 2003; de Bekker-Grob et al. 2012). In applying stated preference methods one confronts all the challenges of survey research, as well as some challenges specific to eliciting willingness to pay for or accept hypothetical changes in the quantity or quality of a good (Boardman et al. 2011). Most of the elicitation challenges are manifestations of findings from behavioral economics. Over the last 30 years, environmental economists have improved the craft of stated preference methods by recognizing and responding to these concerns. Indeed, one might argue that behavioral economics has had its greatest influence on policy analysis through its integration into stated preference methods.

The practical application of CBA, especially in the RIA process, often employs the "ingredients method," which involves identifying the various impacts of policies and valuing them with shadow prices, which are marginal social values derived from the existing body of research. For example, based on numerous studies in many different contexts, transportation economists generally use one-half the wage rate as an estimate of the marginal social value of changes in commuting time (Zhang et al. 2004; US Department of Transportation 2014a). The predicted impacts, or ingredients, are based on a variety of methods, sometimes including evaluations of similar policies. Relevant shadow prices for valuing them are often derived from market analogy or stated preference methods. The benefits of the policy are estimated as the sum of the valued impacts. The strength of this approach depends both on the accuracy of the prediction of impacts and the plausibility of the shadow prices.

Opportunity cost can often be predicted based on estimates of the quantities of resources that will be needed to implement a policy and the market prices of those resources. This is typically the case for infrastructure projects (assuming that environmental impacts are accounted for in the measure of benefits). The prediction may be less certain when the policy allows firms or individuals to satisfy requirements with combinations of resources that they choose. Valuation issues arise when inputs are not traded in undistorted markets. For example, a classic problem for analysts arises in valuing labor used for a project when law or custom places a floor on wages that creates involuntary unemployment (Haveman and Weimer 2015).

The final step shown in Figure 2.2 involves predicting net benefits as the difference between social benefits (typically from the ingredients method but possibly from one of the earlier steps) and social costs (based on the opportunity costs of the resources needed to implement the policy).

The discussion summarized in Figure 2.1 places CBA into the perspective of public policy analysis in which it provides a protocol for assessing the almost always important, but rarely singular, goal of efficiency. It brings into question the wisdom of any proposals to build distributional values into CBA, as doing so would likely obscure tradeoffs between efficiency and other important public policy goals by submerging them into a single measure. CBA does sufficient and useful work by providing a protocol for systematically comparing the efficiency of policy alternatives.

Yet, as should be clear from the discussion summarized in Figure 2.2, the assessment of efficiency through CBA requires both conceptual and practical expediencies. The next section introduces additional expediencies related to uncertainty about, and the timing of, costs and benefits. Noting that CBA assess efficiency only imperfectly within the framework of neoclassical economics helps set realistic expectations for any guidelines for how CBA should assess efficiency within the broader and less unified framework of behavioral economics.

BEHAVIORALLY CONTESTABLE ELEMENTS OF NEOCLASSICAL WELFARE ECONOMICS

Having interpreted CBA broadly within the framework of neoclassical welfare economics, we turn now to some of its key elements that are contested by behavioral economics. The task is best accomplished with some formalization.

UTILITY AND EXPENDITURE FUNCTIONS

The starting point for neoclassical analysis is the assumption that each individual has a utility function that depends on the bundle of goods consumed, such that higher values of the function indicate more preferred bundles:

$$U = u(x_1, x_2, \ldots, x_K; q_1, q_2, \ldots, q_J) \qquad \text{(EQ. 2.1)}$$

where x_k is the amount of the kth private good consumed and where q_j is the quantity of the jth public good consumed—the former are goods such as apples that are rivalrous in consumption, and the latter are goods such as air quality that are non-rivalrous in the sense that everyone in the locality consumes the same level of the good without diminishing consumption of the good for others. In the standard formulation, these are the quantities of goods consumed by the individual herself. One could also allow the person to be altruistic (other-regarding) by expanding the arguments to include the consumption of goods by others and still derive the metrics for utility changes that follow. Indeed, one could also imagine the person having preferences over public goods such as the distribution of income in society or even over collective processes (process regarding), such as the way public decisions are made. Again, the metrics for utility changes would carry over if these "moral sentiments" can be expressed as arguments in the utility function (Zerbe 2004).

The problem facing the individual is to maximize U when the price of private good x_k is p_k and the person has an income B_o. (Assume that the q_j^o are exogenously determined by public policy.) The individual chooses values x_k^o to maximize U subject to the budget constraint imposed by current income, B_o:

$$\sum_{k=1}^{K} p_k x_k^o = B_o \qquad \text{(EQ. 2.2)}$$

Label the resulting utility U_o. An expenditure function is defined as the amount of income needed to achieve some level of utility for given prices and quantities of public goods. The maximization of utility by the individual with the initial set of prices and utility implies the following expenditure function, e:

$$B_o = e_{oo}(p_I^o, r, p_K^o; q_I^o, \ldots, q_J^o; U_o) \qquad \text{(EQ. 2.3)}$$

where the first subscript of e indicates the initial prices and public good quantities and the second indicates the initial level of utility.

The compensating variation, CV, for a policy that would, say, change the quantity of the first public good from q_I^o to q_I^I would be written as:

$$CV \equiv B_o - e_{Io}(p_I^o, \ldots, p_K^o; q_I^I, \ldots, q_J^o; U_o) \qquad \text{(EQ. 2.4)}$$

where the first subscript of e indicates the new prices and public good quantities and second subscript the original utility level. That is, the CV is the change in income that would give the individual utility U_o after the change in the quantity of the public good. If the change in q_I makes the person better off, then less than B_o in income would be needed to achieve utility U_o and the CV would be positive. If the change makes the person worse off, then more than B_o in income would be needed to achieve utility U_o and the CV would be negative.

The equivalent variation, EV, is measured relative to the utility, U_I, that would result after the change if income remained constant. EV would be the change in income that would be needed to achieve U_I in the absence of the change in q_I:

$$EV \equiv e_{oI}(p_I^o, \ldots, p_K^o; q_I^o, \ldots, q_J^o; U_I) - B_o \qquad \text{(EQ. 2.5)}$$

where the first subscript of e indicates the original prices and public good quantities and the second subscript the new utility that would result from the new prices and public good quantities at the original income level. If the increase in q_I makes the person better off, then U_I is higher than U_o and the value of the expenditure function in Equation 2.5 will be larger than B_o because more income would be needed with current prices and public goods quantities to reach U_I. If the increase in q_I makes the person worse off, then U_I is lower than U_o and the value of the expenditure function will be smaller than B_o because less income would be needed with current prices and public goods quantities to reach U_I.

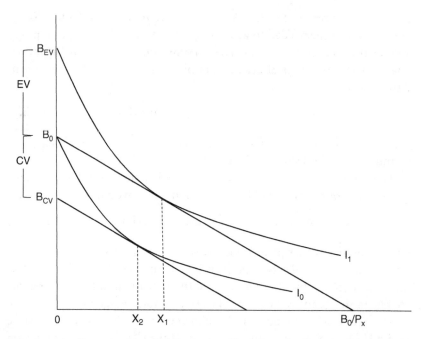

FIGURE 2.3 Compensating and Equivalent Variations for Opening Market for X

Note that the definitions of CV and EV hold for multiple changes in prices (say, either exogenously through excise taxes or endogenously through changes in prices for complements and substitutes of the good directly affected by policy), multiple changes in public good quantities, or combinations of price and public good changes. In such cases, the calculation of e_{10} and U_1 would be based on the full set of changes, including both those that result directly from the policy change and those that result as individuals adjust their consumption of private goods and thereby possibly change market prices.

Figure 2.3 shows CV and EV graphically for a policy that would introduce a market for good X that previously did not exist—say, either because government had not provided appropriate property rights to support it or because government had banned it outright. The vertical axis is the amount of money the consumer has available to spend on all goods. In the absence of the market, she cannot purchase any X so she spends her entire income, B_0, on other goods. This is represented by the point $(0, B_0)$ on the graph. The collection of all combinations of consumption of X and expenditure amounts on other things that would give the consumer that same utility as $(0, B_0)$ is represented as the indifference curve labeled I_0. That is, she would be indifferent among the combinations of X and expenditure on other things represented by points on I_o. Now imagine government adopts a policy that would create a market in which X sells for price P_x. She can now choose any point on the budget constraint line connecting the points (o, B_o) and $(B_o/P_x, o)$, where the latter point would involve her spending the entire budget on X. The introduction of the market now allows her to move to any point on the budget constraint line. To maximize utility, she would select the point on the budget line that is just tangent to the "highest" possible indifference curve, I_1, offering the highest level of utility. This would be point $(X_1, B_o-P_xX_1)$.

The CV for this policy change would answer the question: If the market is introduced, how much could the consumer's budget be reduced so that she would have the same utility as she had before the market was introduced? The answer to this question can be found in two steps: First, reduce the consumer's budget to B_{CV} so that the budget constraint line is just tangential to the initial indifference curve I_o. This would result in the point $(X_2, B_{CV}-P_xX_2)$. Second, CV equals the difference between the original budget, B_o, and B_{CV}.

The EV for this policy change would answer the question: How much would the consumer's budget have to be increased instead of introducing the market so that she would have the same utility as she would have had had the market been introduced? Again, the answer can be found in two steps. First, increase the consumer's budget to B_{EV} so that she can reach I_o without the market. Second, EV equals the difference between B_{EV} and B_o. As an aside, note that all policies that resulted in consumption at points on I_1 would have the same EV, but not necessarily the same CV—a reason why some economists argue for choosing EV rather than CV as the primary measure of welfare change despite its less intuitive interpretation.

The construction of CV and EV require three assumptions that will be relevant to our subsequent discussion of behavioral economics. I label these (and similar assumptions identified subsequently) as "behavioral-economics relevant assumptions," or BERA.

BERA1: The functional form of utility remains constant over the period of assessment. That is, utility only depends on the arguments of the function and not on any other contextual factors that may vary.

BERA2: The individual chooses consumption bundles so as to maximize utility. Therefore, because of BERA1, the choices the individual makes actually maximize the utility experienced. In other words, there is no difference between what can be called decision utility, the basis for choice, and experienced utility, the level of satisfaction that actually results.

BERA3: The utility of a bundle of goods depends only on the levels of those goods and not on any prior or future allocation. CV and EV obviously depend on the status quo allocation, but utilities used to calculate them depend only on the amounts actually consumed. In other words, utility depends only on consumption and not on consumption relative to some starting, or reference, point.

RISK, EXPECTED UTILITY, AND UPDATING

Many important public policies involve uncertain outcomes: construction of levees to protect against the collective risk of flooding; smoking cessation programs to reduce the individual risk of disease; pre-school programs for children from low-income families to increase the chance of high-school completion. To address the efficiency of policies that have uncertain outcomes, neoclassical economics generally employs two simplifications. First, the uncertainty is characterized as risk by assuming either a complete or at least a representative set of possible outcomes and the assignment of a probability of occurrence to each element of the set. These geminated outcomes and probabilities comprise a prospect, or a lottery. For example, the flip of a fair coin is a lottery that has the outcome heads with a probability of one-half and the outcome tails with a probability of one-half. Each probability must be greater than or equal to zero and less than or equal to one and the probabilities must sum to exactly one. Second, individuals facing risk are assumed to act as if they are maximizing expected utility, the so-called expected utility hypothesis, introduced by von Neumann and Morgenstern (1944).

Imagine a consumer facing two alternative actions, 1 and 2, with different prospects, or lotteries, over outcomes. Further, imagine that the set of possible outcomes from choice 1, y_1, y_2, ..., y_n, would occur with probabilities v_1, v_2, ..., v_n, respectively, and that the set of possible outcomes from choice 2, z_1, z_2, ..., z_m, would occur with probabilities w_1, w_2, ..., w_m, respectively. The expected utility of alternative 1 would be

$$U_1 = v_1 U(y_1) + \cdots + v_n U(y_n) \qquad \text{(EQ. 2.6)}$$

and the expected utility of alternative 2 would be

$$U_2 = w_1 U(z_1) + \cdots + w_m U(z_m) \qquad \text{(EQ. 2.7)}$$

By the expected utility hypothesis, the individual would choose alternative 1 over alternative 2 if $U_1 > U_2$, or alternative 2 over alternative 1 if $U_2 > U_1$. If $U_1 = U_2$, then the individual would be indifferent between the alternatives.

The theorem underlying this hypothesis can be proven to hold if a number of axioms are satisfied. First, individuals must have complete and transitive preference relations over the possible outcomes. Second, individuals resolve compound lotteries (lotteries with lotteries as prizes) into simple lotteries over the possible outcomes with probabilities computed according to the ordinary laws of probability. Third, for some probability p, if lottery L_1 is preferred to lottery L_2, then the lottery $pL_1 + (1-p)L_3$ is preferred to the lottery $pL_2 + (1-p)L_3$. This third axiom, commonly referred to as the independence axiom, requires that the expected utilities be computed as linear in the probabilities (Machina 1987). If the independence axiom, or either of the other axioms, does not hold, then the theorem cannot be proved so that larger expected utility does not necessarily indicate a more preferred alternative.

In most circumstances, but especially in situations involving collective risk, the most appropriate approach for taking account of outcome uncertainty in CBA is the measurement of benefit to the individual through option price, the maximum amount an individual would be willing to pay for certain for a policy with uncertain outcomes (Boardman et al. 2011). The option price, which does not depend on which outcome actually occurs, can be compared directly with the cost of the policy, which also usually does not depend on which outcome actually occurs. The definition of option price depends on the expected utility hypothesis (Graham 1981). Although option price can be elicited directly through stated preference methods, it usually requires very strong assumptions to impute from revealed preference data.

An alternative, and most commonly used, approach to measuring benefits when outcomes are uncertain is to calculate an expected value for the benefits over the possible outcomes. Like the expected utility hypothesis, this approach requires linearity in probabilities. However, it is even stronger than the expected utility hypothesis because it also implies risk neutrality: it treats as equally beneficial certain and uncertain projects if the expected benefit of the latter equals the benefit of the former. For policies that reduce (increase) income risk, it will be smaller (larger) than option price. The difference between option price and the expected benefit is the policy's option value, which is usually a non-quantified benefit when expected benefits rather than option price is the basis for measuring benefits.

The expected utility hypothesis has a fundamental role in neoclassical prediction and valuation. Its use embeds a number of behavioral-economics relevant assumptions:

BERA4: Individuals correctly interpret and employ probabilities in their decisions.

BERA5: Individuals employ probabilities linearly in assessing the utility of alternatives with uncertain outcomes.

Individuals learn from their experience. In situations of uncertainty, the learning can take the form of updated estimates of the probabilities of outcomes. Indeed, many policies seek to help individuals make better assessments of probabilities by providing them with relevant information. Individuals maximizing expected utility are assumed to follow the basic principles of probability theory. In particular, they are expected to incorporate new information into their probability estimates through Bayes' rule:

$$P(A|B) = P(B|A)P(A)/P(B) \qquad \text{(EQ. 2.8)}$$

where A and B are two events, $P(A)$ is the individual's subjective probability that A will occur before any new information is available (the prior probability), $P(B|A)$ is the probability that B will be observed given that A occurs, $P(B)$ is the probability that B will occur, and $P(A|B)$ is the new subjective (posterior) probability of A occurring after receiving the information that B has occurred. For example, A may be the likelihood of breast cancer, $P(A)$ is an estimate of the probability based on age and family background, B is a positive mammogram (suspicious or suggestive of malignancy), $P(B|A)$ is the probability of a positive mammogram given that breast cancer is present, and $P(B)$ is the probability of a positive mammogram, which depends on the characteristics of the test and the prior probability of cancer.

BERA6: Individuals follow the laws of probability, including Bayes' rule, in updating their estimates of the probabilities of uncertain outcomes.

MULTIPLE TIME PERIODS AND PRESENT VALUES

Public policies often have benefits and costs that accrue over extended periods of time. Infrastructure projects typically require substantial construction costs that accrue in the first year or two, and then annual benefits from use and costs for maintenance that accrue for many years afterward. Similar patterns of initial costs followed by streams of benefits and costs over many years also arise from projects that involve investments in environmental quality or human capital. CBA employs time discounting to convert these streams of benefits and costs into present values that can be summed to arrive at a present value of net benefits for assessing efficiency.

Although consumption in multiple time periods could be accommodated in Equation 2.1 by adding sets of consumption arguments for each of the periods, the resulting utility functions would be too intractable to be of use in practical analysis. Instead, the near universal assumption in empirical research is that global utility, the overall assessment of the value of current and future consumption, can be written as the discounted sum of utilities over relevant periods. Further, it is assumed that the utility in each period depends on consumption in that period valued by a utility function that remains the same across periods. In other words, the global utility function is assumed to be separable into weighted additive terms. The weights indicate the willingness of the individual to trade consumption across periods. Time consistency, the desirable property that, absent changing circumstances, an individual would not want to deviate from a consumption path initially chosen to maximize global utility, requires that weights be exponential. If r is the individual's marginal rate of pure time preference, the rate at which he or she trades consumption between periods, then the global utility, U_G, of a stream of consumption bundles c_0, $c_1, c_2, \ldots, c_N$ is

$$U_G(c_1, c_2, \ldots, c_N) = \sum_{n=0}^{N} \frac{U(c_n)}{(1+r)^n} \qquad \text{(EQ. 2.9)}$$

where $U(c_n)$ is the utility for period n.

BERA7: Individuals have a marginal rate of pure time preference that they use in the exponential discounting of future consumption.

Table 2.1 lists the seven BERA discussed in this section. It also indicates the chapters in which each of the BERA is particularly relevant to the consideration of behavioral implications for CBA.

TABLE 2.1 *Behaviorally Relevant Assumptions (BERA) of Neoclassical Welfare: Statements and Chapters in Which They Are Challenged*

1. The functional form of utility remains constant over the period of assessment. That is, it only depends on the arguments of the function and not on any other contextual factors that may vary. (Chapters 3 and 4)
2. The individual chooses consumption bundles so as to maximize utility. Therefore, because of BERA1, the choices the individual makes actually maximize the utility experienced. (Chapters 3 and 4)
3. The utility of a bundle of goods depends only on the levels of those goods and not on any prior or future allocation. CV and EV obviously depend on the status quo allocation, but utilities used to calculate them do not. (Chapters 5 and 7)
4. Individuals correctly interpret and employ probabilities in their decisions. (Chapters 4 and 7)
5. Individuals employ probabilities linearly in assessing the utility of alternatives with uncertain outcomes. (Chapter 4)
6. Individuals follow the laws of probability, including Bayes' rule, in updating their estimates of the probabilities of uncertain outcomes. (Chapter 4)
7. Individuals have a marginal rate of pure time preference that they use in the exponential discounting of future consumption. (Chapters 6 and 7)

CONCLUSION

CBA should be viewed as a protocol for assessing the relative economic efficiency of policy alternatives. Except in the rare case that economic efficiency is the only relevant social goal, CBA is not an appropriate decision rule. Recognizing that its primary role is in assessing the relative efficiency of policy alternatives within a multi-goal framework appropriately focuses attention on how well it does so. This chapter briefly reviews the ethical, technical, and practical concerns that arise in moving from a Pareto improvement to an actual assessment of net benefits to set the context for considering the challenges that behavioral economics poses for CBA through its evidence of violations of the BERA. We now turn to addressing the challenges these violations pose for CBA, first from the perspective of the proposed behavioral alternatives to neoclassical welfare economics, and then from the perspective of violations of specific BERA.

3

Possible Behavioral Frameworks for CBA

Neoclassical welfare economics relies on a number of assumptions challenged by the empirical findings of behavioral economics. Policy analysts would welcome a revised welfare economics that relaxes or replaces the challenged assumptions but still provides a basis for valuing the impacts of public policies in terms of their relative efficiencies—that is, how well they use scarce resources to facilitate valued consumption. Scholars have proposed a number of approaches for integrating behavioral findings into neoclassical welfare economics. Although frameworks proposed by Sugden (2004), Bernheim and Rangel (2007 and 2009), and Bernheim (2016) accommodate behavioral findings in intellectually coherent ways, they do not directly provide the adequate practical guidance needed for actually doing CBA (Smith and Moore 2010; Brennan 2014). Nonetheless, they provide some valuable conceptual resources for the less comprehensive, but practical, approaches to specific behavioral challenges that I seek to develop.

Our primary concern is the valuation of the efficiency impacts of public policies. If the findings of behavioral economics were only relevant to the prediction of behavior, then it would pose neither a conceptual nor a practical problem for CBA. Analysts should use whatever theories, models, and empirical evidence enables them to make the best possible predictions of policy impacts. When behavioral economics, or any social science theory or evidence for that matter, provides a better prediction of policy-relevant impacts than neoclassical economics, it should be used. This is worth stating as a guideline:

PGL 3.1 *Use whatever theory, behavioral or otherwise, that provides the best predictions of policy impacts.*

The predictions, however, must be valued so as to allow for the assessment of efficiency. In some cases, a clear distinction between prediction and valuation can be preserved so that the principles of neoclassical welfare economics can be employed to monetize impacts predicted by whatever means. In other cases, the predictions based on behavioral economics either raise questions about the principles of neoclassical valuation or make their appropriate application ambiguous (Gowdy 2004).

The following sections briefly review three approaches for accommodating the findings of behavioral economics within CBA. The first, and most incremental, approach preserves the assumption that individuals have coherent preferences. However, they sometimes do not act according to them because they fail to make an accurate assessment of their own future preference or because they simply misperceive how consumption will satisfy their preferences. The second approach—and the most radical departure from neoclassical welfare economics—is the proposal of Sugden (2004, 2005) to shift the normative focus of economics away from choice to opportunity. The third, developed by Bernheim and Rangel (2007, 2009), attempts to preserve the choice-theoretic basis of neoclassical welfare economics by introducing ancillary conditions about the circumstances of choice that allow for the observed incoherencies revealed by behavioral research. Although allowing for choices that fail to satisfy true underlying preferences offers several expedient avenues for responding to the behavioral challenges to CBA, the comprehensive frameworks developed by Sugden and especially by Bernheim and Rangel potentially offer more general principles for dealing with incoherent preferences.

CHOICES INCONSISTENT WITH "TRUE" PREFERENCES

The applied tools of neoclassical welfare analysis assume that the individual has coherent preferences that can be represented as a stable utility function (BERA1 in Chapter 2) and that the choices the individual makes reveal those preferences (BERA2 through BERA7, also in Chapter 2). When choices are inconsistent with preferences (violations of any BERA2 through BERA7), but the preferences are nonetheless well defined (BERA1 holds), then it may be possible to predict policy impacts on the basis of observed choices and then value the impacts using the "true" utility function. Of course, if "true" preferences cannot be inferred from the choices that provide the empirical basis for prediction, then the "true" utility function must be discovered by some other means, such as the observation of decisions in other circumstances that do reveal it.

When individuals do not choose among alternatives as if they are maximizing some stable utility function, their choices may reveal incoherence. The earliest demonstrations of individuals often making systematically incoherent choices were in situations involving risk where the expected utility hypothesis (BERA5) appears not to hold. Such incoherence has been most troubling theoretically because it indicates a violation of instrumental rationality. Of particular concern are intransitive revealed preferences: a is preferred to b and b is preferred to c, but c is preferred to a, or defining the binary preference relation xPy as meaning x is preferred to y, aPbPcPa. Such intransitivity creates the opportunity for exploiting a so-called money pump that would allow a rational trader to extract payments from the individual with intransitive preferences for providing moves from a to c and from c to b and from b back to a and so on. However, from a public policy perspective, we may also care about choices that violate substantive rationality (Sen 1990; Kahneman 1994)—that is, choices that do not actually maximize utility whether or not they reveal intransitivity or other incoherence.

DECISION UTILITY VERSUS EXPERIENCED UTILITY

A potentially useful distinction can be made between *decision utility* and *experienced utility* (Kahneman and Thaler 1991; Kahneman 1994). Consider an individual making a decision now that will produce consequences revealed sometime in the future. Consistent with neoclassical assumptions, assume that the individual will experience a level of utility that depends on the consequences that actually occur from the choice. However, also assume that the individual must predict this experienced utility at the time of the decision and make a choice that maximizes it. If prediction is imperfect, then there may be a divergence between the choices based on maximizing the predicted, or decision utility, and the choices that would have been made to maximize experienced utility. The greater the imperfection, the more likely it is that the choices actually made will fail to maximize experienced utility.

The psychology and behavioral economics literatures identify a number of cognitive processes and choice circumstances that systematically hinder the accurate prediction of experienced utility. Kahneman and Thaler (2006) refer to the prediction of experienced utility as "hedonic forecasts." Forecasting error tends to be larger the more the emotional state and the circumstances of the individual differ between the time the decision is made and the time the consequences of the decision are experienced. As emotional states and circumstances are more likely to differ the longer the time between decision and experience, greater delays tend to contribute to greater forecasting error.

Passive acceptance of defaults, lack of relevant experience, and choice complexity are "red flags" that revealed preferences are errors in the sense of not corresponding to individuals' true interests (Beshears et al. 2008). Purely random hedonic forecasting errors do not necessarily pose a serious problem for applied neoclassical welfare analysis. Random utility models separate the variables affecting utility into those that are observable and those that are unobservable but random. So, for example, in terms of variables such as style and fuel efficiency, someone might prefer one model of automobile over another. However, there may be unobservable factors, such as the mood of the individual at the time of purchase, that lead her to choose the other model. If these unobservable factors can be represented as the realization of a random variable unrelated to the observable factors, likely reasonable when looking across a set of actual choices, then the random utility model is a plausible basis for predicting behavior. Random utilities were central to the pioneering development of conditional logit models of qualitative choice by Daniel McFadden (1974), and underlie much revealed preference and almost all stated preference analyses (Haab and McConnell 2003). Analyses of data generated from random utility models take advantage of repeated observations, typically across individuals, to average out the random component to recover the effects of observable variables. However, non-random forecasting error potentially causes a more serious practical problem because it creates the risk of statistical analyses confounding the effects of the observable variables with the unobservable variables driving the non-random error.

Kahneman and Thaler (2006) review the sources of error in hedonic forecasts within four general categories, to which one could add a fifth. First, errors may arise if individuals assess their future experience in terms of their current emotions and motivations rather than the emotions and motivations they are likely to have when they experience the consequences of their decisions. In particular, current emotions and motivations are likely to anchor the projected emotions and motivations, resulting in "projection bias" (Loewenstein et al. 2003). For example, very hungry grocery shoppers are likely to purchase different foods and in larger quantities than they would if they were less hungry while shopping. If most of their actual consumption of the groceries will be in a less hungry state, then they likely have made purchases that will not maximize the value they actually obtain from them when preparing meals later in the week.

Second, errors may arise if the circumstances of choice focus attention on attributes of the outcome that will not be as important in experiencing it. One often relevant circumstance is whether alternatives are evaluated in comparison to other goods or alone. Comparisons tend to focus attention on differences that may not be relevant when the alternative is experienced. For example, comparison of automobiles in terms of standard accessories may focus attention on their audio systems even though the quality of the audio system may be relatively unimportant to the person when she is actually operating the vehicle. Even when comparisons are not required for the valuation, the presentation of other goods with the one being evaluated may influence that evaluation (Morewedge et al. 2010). For example, seeing a compact car in a showroom with sedans may result in a different hedonic forecast for it than if it were viewed in a showroom with other compacts. With respect to sequences of consumption, making choices simultaneously may result in a selection of different alternatives than would be selected sequentially. For instance, a person asked to select breakfasts from a menu for the next three days might select three different breakfasts, but if given the choice each day might instead select the same item each day. Such excessive variety-seeking in simultaneous choice is referred to as diversification bias (Read and Loewenstein 1995).

Third, errors may arise if decisions are made on the basis of incorrect inferences from past experiences. The ease with which one can recall events may depend on their salience, distorting predictions of causality through what has been called the availability heuristic (Tversky and Kahneman 1974). When people assess their own experiences, they often seem to neglect the duration of those experiences (Varey and Kahneman 1992; Do et al. 2008). In particular, rather than placing equal or time-discounted weight on extended experiences, people appear to be following the so-called peak/end rule, recalling the pain or pleasure of the experience as an average of its most intense level and its final level (Kahneman et al. 1997). For example, in the case of painful medical treatments, people tend to place weight on the most intense pain and the pain at the end of the treatment, ignoring the duration and intensity of pain between these points. Thus, although past experience potentially allows for more informed hedonic forecasts, the availability and duration biases may contribute to divergence between decision and experienced utility.

Fourth, people often fail to anticipate how they would adapt to changes in life circumstances. People tend to be subject to a focusing illusion that leads them to overemphasize any particular aspect of life that they happen to be considering in thinking about the future (Schkade and Kahneman 1998). For example, asking sighted people about the impact that they would expect blindness to have on their lives suggests that they would suffer a dramatic decline in their quality of life, while those who are blind typically report a much smaller impact. Consistent with this argument, a study that compared multiple sclerosis patients with the general population found that the former were less willing to bear additional mortality risk to avoid multiple sclerosis than the former (Sloan et al. 1998). Some researchers have interpreted such differences in terms of happiness (Kahneman and Sugden 2005; Loewenstein and Ubel 2008), which, inappropriately from the perspective of CBA, diverts attention from the measures we employ to monetize changes in utility. The relevant CBA questions are not about happiness, but rather about the willingness to make tradeoffs. The sighted person would be asked a question about willingness to accept blindness while the blind person would be asked a question about willingness to pay for sightedness. Nonetheless, among the various explanations for the often observed difference between willingness to accept and willingness to pay, the focusing illusion may play a role.

A fifth source of error in hedonic forecasts arises from errors in dealing with uncertainty. In addition to the long-recognized biases that arise when people employ heuristics to estimate and employ probabilities (Tversky and Kahneman 1974), individuals also seem prone to overconfidence. In particular, they tend to show over-optimism by predicting too likely or too large positive outcomes, and over-precision by underestimating the variation in possible outcomes (Malmendier and Taylor 2015). Such overconfidence has been found in studies of consumer behavior (Grubb 2015). For example, individuals appear to be overconfident about their use of athletic club facilities and often choose long-term contracts when per visit payments would be less expensive (DellaVigna and Malmendier 2006). Research also finds considerable overconfidence among investors (Daniel and Hirshleifer 2015).

The divergence between decision utility and experienced utility because of hedonic forecasting errors argues for choosing policies that maximize the latter despite the individual making choices that reveal the former

(Chetty 2015). Yet, if experienced utility cannot be observed directly from behavior based on decision utility, then how can it be discovered? Surveys that ask people about their subjective happiness after they experience consumption do not provide a useful basis for estimating willingness to pay or accept. Further, these subjective measures may be subject to some of the same perceptional problems that give rise to hedonic forecasting error (Carter and McBride 2013; Adler 2016). Information to help estimate experienced utility might come from experiments and observational studies that varied the context from one that matched the decision situation to one that reduced hedonic forecasting errors—for example, comparing the actual choice situation in which policy has an impact with one in which people have help in using information to deal with uncertainty. It may also be possible to develop shadow prices to help adjust for particular behavioral anomalies. For example, including taxes in posted prices appears to depress demand even though the actual price to the consumer does not change (Chetty et al. 2009). If replications were to yield similar results, then the combined empirical evidence could be used to estimate a plausible shadow price for adjusting demand to reflect the price actually paid (experienced) by consumers. The more systematic and robust behavioral anomalies, the more feasible it should be to develop such shadow prices.

It is important to make clear a normative assumption that underlies analyses in subsequent chapters: allocations of resources should be valued in terms of people's experienced utility. Decisions themselves may elicit either positive or negative feelings that differ from those arising from the actual consumption of goods. A comprehensive hedonic analysis would take account of the feeling surrounding decisions. However, CBA seeks only to promote an efficient allocation of resources, which requires a focus on actual consumption. From this perspective, hedonic forecasting errors are indeed errors. Decision utility predicts behavior, but experienced utility provides the appropriate basis for valuing it.

MULTIPLE SELVES: INTERNALITIES

The idea of multiple selves arises from the observation that people sometimes try to constrain their current selves to protect their future selves (Schelling 1984). Viewing individuals as multiple selves may be useful in understanding choices that appear time-inconsistent because of non-exponential discounting (violation of BERA7) or substantively questionable because current consumption involves harmful addiction. If a current choice involves a transaction that inflicts costs on a non-consenting party, then we would say that it involves a negative externality. In the context of multiple selves, a current choice that inflicts future costs on the chooser involves a negative "internality" (Herrnstein et al. 1993).

In contrast to the failure to predict experienced utility accurately, the multiple-selves framework assumes that the current self knows the utility of future selves but fails to make choices that maximize the present value of utility realized by all the selves. The divergence often results from present-biased preferences (O'Donoghue and Rabin 1999, 103): "When considering trade-offs between two future moments, present-biased preferences give stronger relative weight to the earlier moment as it gets closer." Such present-biased preferences are inconsistent with maximizing the present value of utility based on exponential discounting. For example, Jonathan Gruber and Botond Köszegi (2001) show how hyperbolic discounting can result in smokers imposing internalities on their future selves. In the presence of internalities, it may be possible for government intervention to increase the present value of utility even in the absence of externalities. It is important, however, to distinguish between hyperbolic discounting and simply a high discount rate. For example, smokers may be employing exponential discounting, but with a relative high discount rate (Scharff and Viscusi 2011).

Intertemporal neoclassical economic models make utility a function of consumption in the current and all future periods. In practice, utility is defined for the current and each future period and exponentially discounted back to the current periods. Some critics have argued that the present value perspective privileges the current period. In the context of the multiple selves, the maximization of present values seems to make the current self a dictator, in the sense of making decisions in which future selves do not have a voice. Some theorists, particularly those concerned with the meaning of sustainability, have argued that normative analysis should be based on the principle of non-dictatorship (Chichilnisky 1996). That is, no one self should be able to choose consumption for all the selves. In reality, however, individual choices do fall to the current self. How should these choices be assessed normatively?

The non-dictatorship principle suggests that welfare analysis should treat the multiple selves as if they were different individuals with equal standing. In this spirit, Eric Rasmusen (2012) proposes the *interself Kaldor–Hicks criterion*: a policy change is efficient if the winners from the change would be willing to compensate the losers fully. For example, ignoring interpersonal externalities, a policy that improved adolescent diet by reducing access to tasty but unhealthy foods would be efficient if the adult selves would be willing to pay a sufficient amount to compensate the adolescent self for the reduced access.

To apply the interself Kaldor–Hicks criterion in CBA, it must be possible to estimate willingness to pay and willingness to accept for the different selves. The great foresight and massive resources required to do so generally preclude the assembly of longitudinal data to make these estimates through intra-personal analysis. Rather, more feasible methods would likely be based on contemporaneous data for individuals in different generations, raising issues of comparability. Nonetheless, the interself Kaldo–Hicks criterion may provide guidance in thinking about how to accommodate violations of the neoclassical assumptions about intertemporal choice if one rejects the objective of maximizing welfare from the perspective of the current self.

OPPORTUNITY RATHER THAN PREFERENCE SATISFACTION

Recognizing the essential role of coherent preferences (including BERA1 and BERA2) in the valuations underlying Pareto efficiency, Robert Sugden (2004) sees the apparent incoherencies in preferences revealed by research in behavioral economics as a fundamental challenge to neoclassical welfare economics. He proposes an ingenious but radical reframing of welfare economics to focus on the normative criterion of maximization of opportunity rather than maximization of preference satisfaction. The essence of the change is viewing individuals not as necessarily having coherent preferences, but rather as being responsible for whatever choices they make. In this framing, giving individuals more consumption opportunities, whether or not they coherently choose among them, is a desirable social goal: "if an individual is understood as a continuing locus of responsibility, any increase in that individual's lifetime opportunity is good for her in an unambiguous sense" (Sugden 2004, 1018).

As an analog for, and replacement of, Pareto efficiency, he proposes a criterion for assessing the allocation of opportunities. Like Pareto efficiency, it is based on the inability to increase opportunities for one person without decreasing them for someone else: "for every feasible alternative to the actual outcome, *someone* can take responsibility for that alternative not having come about" (Sugden 2004, 1020). As in neoclassical economics, this approach gives sovereignty to consumers. Indeed, it respects them as sovereign without also requiring that they have stable preferences and the capability to make choices that best satisfy those preferences. Thus, whereas some scholars see behavioral economics as a justification for public policies to help consumers make "better" choices (Thaler and Sunstein 2003, 2008), Sugden (2008, 2009) rejects such paternalistic overriding of consumer choices as unnecessary for, or even inconsistent with, the maximization of opportunity.

Sugden (2004) lays the foundation for his argument by proposing an analog to the first welfare theorem of neoclassical economics: just as the competitive economy achieves Pareto efficiency in terms of satisfying preferences under neoclassical assumptions, the market economy satisfies the opportunity criterion under a few less restrictive assumptions. He proves the theorem for an exchange economy (fixed quantities of all available goods) under the following substantive assumptions: First, although consumers do not necessarily have coherent preferences, when given the option of buying a good at two prices, they buy at the lower price, and when given the option of selling a good at two prices, they sell at the higher price. Second, there are a large number of fully rational traders whose sole objective is to maximize their money holdings. Third, at the beginning of each trading period, each trader sets four quantities for each non-money good: a selling price, a buying price, the maximum quantity to be sold, and the maximum quantity to be bought. In addition, there are a few technical assumptions needed for the proof.

Sugden defines a free-entry equilibrium as an analog to the neoclassical competitive equilibrium: a configuration of offers by traders is a free-entry equilibrium if no trader trades at a loss and no non-active trader can make a positive profit by entering the market. Assuming a large number of consumers, a free-entry equilibrium will involve either a buying price or a selling price for each non-money good that allows all requests by consumers to buy or sell at that price to be met. His welfare theorem is that the free-entry equilibrium satisfies the opportunity criterion. That is, the interaction of the less than fully rational consumers (they are not constrained to make coherent exchanges during the trading period, only to be price sensitive) with the fully rational traders results in an equilibrium in which it would not be possible to increase the consumption opportunities for one consumer without decreasing the consumption opportunities for at least one other consumer.

To accept Sugden's reframing of welfare economics, one must also accept the individual as a continuing locus of responsibility so that the higher ranking of allocations with greater opportunity is unequivocally desirable. A number of common situations would likely make many people reject this starting point of continuous responsibility. For example, many cigarette smokers begin smoking in their teens as a result of peer pressure, myopia, experimentation, or a desire to appear more adult. In view of the strong addictive property of nicotine, the teenage choice to smoke makes it much more costly, perhaps prohibitively so, to stop smoking as an adult. How is the opportunity criterion to be applied in such a case? Would a policy that prevented teenage smoking be a reduction in opportunity even if it made not smoking as an adult a more widespread opportunity? Perhaps one might restrict the assumption of responsibility to adults, but then we face the tricky question of where to draw the line between adolescence and adulthood.

Or consider situations in which many individuals can only learn about irreversible consequences through experience. For example, discovering the full range of consequences of a food supplement prior to consumption may be practically impossible for someone without epidemiological training. Preserving the opportunity to consume the supplement may result in some consumers with unexpected heart attacks that end their loci of responsibility. In the neoclassical framework, this situation might be framed as an inefficiency resulting from an information asymmetry: the purveyors of the supplement know more about its consequences than do most consumers. A natural policy remedy to consider would be a requirement for the purveyors of the supplement to provide consumers with information about the risks of taking it. However, if consumers are unable to interpret the risks, and there are less risky alternatives providing similar benefits, then a ban might very well maximize net benefits in the neoclassical framework, but it would seem to reduce opportunity. Problems with the same structure can arise in personal finance, where the consequence of bankruptcy may not be reversible, or in building vulnerable structures in earthquake or flood zones, where unlucky outcomes can cause catastrophic individual and collective harm.

One can also question whether the free-entry model adequately takes account of incoherent preferences. During the trading period when incoherent preferences are revealed, the trades do not result in actual consumption, but rather in temporary holdings of the goods. Only the preferences expressed when equilibrium is reached result in consumption. Incoherent preferences expressed during the trading period affect the final allocation by changing endowments as the equilibrium is approached, but do not capture consumption along a path that actually reduces the total amount of the good available.

Perhaps less fundamental, but certainly more practically important, neoclassical welfare economics allows us to assess the relative efficiency of policy changes that are not Pareto improving through the Kaldor–Hicks criterion. Determination of potential Pareto improvement is possible because assumed preference coherence allows for the assessment of consumption changes in terms of money metrics that can be summed across individuals. With the various caveats discussed in Chapter 2, we have a way of comparing policies that increase consumption by some but decrease it by others. Absent coherent preferences, however, such valuation is problematic, the very concern that motivates this book: for an opportunity set to be unequivocally inferior to another choice set, it must be a proper subset of that set. In situations in which two opportunity sets differ so that one is not a subset of the other, it is not clear within the Sugden framework how they would be ranked. In other words, Sugden provides an analog for Pareto efficiency, but not for potential Pareto improvements, the essential construct for practical CBA.

Although normative concerns and practical limitations prevent the opportunity criterion from being the basis for a useful behaviorally tolerant welfare economics, we may nonetheless gain some insights from it that help guide our development of practical CBA responses to behavioral economics. Fortunately, Sugden (2005) helps us with this task in an article motivated by his theorem but focusing explicitly on accommodating incoherent preferences in CBA. He begins by interpreting the use of CBA within the neoclassical welfare economics paradigm as a guide for finding policies to correct market failures so as to simulate the ideal competitive market to recover its Pareto efficiency. He then argues that the market-clearing price vector in his free-entry equilibrium also achieves Pareto efficiency so that even without the assumption of preference coherence CBA should be directed at simulating the competitive market equilibrium. Further, he argues "that all freely chosen marginal transactions create weakly positive net increases in surplus" (p. 137). Bolstered by the argument that for most goods competitive markets respond to willingness to pay at the moment of consumption, Sugden offers the following principle for valuation:

[B]enefits which accrue to individuals in future periods should be assessed in terms of those individuals' valuations *in the periods in which the benefits accrue,* as predicted by the cost-benefit analyst in the light of the best knowledge currently available to her. In making and acting on such predictions, the analyst's role is analogous to that of the entrepreneur in the model of the ideal market.   (p. 148)

Sugden's principle is both reassuring and surprising. It is reassuring in that it is consistent with the approach that would generally be followed by analysts not taking ad hoc account of behavioral anomalies. That is, consumer surplus provides an appropriate valuation of consumption, and it can be assessed when consumption actually occurs. It is surprising in view of his criticisms of paternalism and nudges, because it requires the analyst to anticipate consumers' future valuations, which may differ from their current valuations. Unfortunately, in view of the particularly narrow way that preference incoherence operates within the free-entry model, the theoretical case for the principle does not seem particularly strong. Thus, Sugden does not provide an unequivocally well-grounded principle for valuation. Nonetheless, his admonition to view the objective of CBA as simulating competitive markets serves as a conceptual resource for addressing preference incoherence.

CHOICE RATHER THAN UNDERLYING PREFERENCE

Rather than abandoning choice for opportunity, B. Douglas Berhiem and Antonio Rangel (2007, 2009) seek to define relations for identifying choices that convey unambiguous information about whether one alternative offers improvement over another. Their generalized choice framework is no less ingenious than Sugden's opportunity criterion, but much less radical. It accommodates diverse decision processes, but reduces to neoclassical welfare economics when choice is based on preference satisfaction. Although it generality requires substantial narrowing assumptions to allow for the actual valuation of alternatives, it nonetheless offers a number of valuable insights to help guide CBA responses to behavioral anomalies.

The generalized choice framework allows individuals to employ a wide range of choice procedures that would result in incoherent revealed preferences. It does so through two of its features. First, it defines a choice object as the particular set of alternatives among which the individual chooses. There exists a set of all possible choice objects. For example, imagine that the alternatives are a, b, and c. The full set of nontrivial choices (that is, the ones actually involving a choice) would be (a,b), (b,c), (a,c), and (a,b,c). Based on the objective knowledge available to the individual, there is a constraint set, X, defined as a subset of all possible choice objects the individual views as feasible. For example, an individual may view (a,c) and (a,b,c) as feasible. In this case, observing the individual choose a from (a,c) and a from (a,b,c) would be consistent with coherent preferences. However, observing the individual choose *a* from (*a*,*c*) and *c* from (*a*,*b*,*c*) would not be consistent with coherent revealed preferences.

Second, it defines a generalized choice situation, G(X,*d*), as a choice set X paired with an ancillary condition *d*. Ancillary conditions, such as the way alternatives or information about them is presented, the designation of an alternative as the status quo, or the particular time at which a decision is made, are aspects of the choice decision that a benevolent planner would not view as relevant to welfare in allocation decisions. Bernheim and Rangel recognize that there is some discretion in drawing the line between the welfare-relevant characteristics of alternatives and the ancillary conditions of choice. However, if all relevant ancillary conditions were made characteristics of choice objects instead, then actual choices would have little or no normative content. As guidance, they propose drawing the line based on the distinction between welfare-relevant characteristics of choice objects and ancillary conditions that would change with the delegation of a decision. The relevant ancillary conditions, and therefore the relevant set of generalized choice situations, would be determined by the positive theory of choice employed by the analyst. For example, neoclassical theory would have no relevant ancillary conditions, while a choice theory involving status quo bias would have ancillary conditions identifying which alternative within each choice object the individual considers the status quo, either inherently or as a result of the received information about the alternatives.

The information available to analysts comes from the choices made by individuals when they face generalized choice situations. To identify the choices, a choice correspondence is defined such that $x \in C(X,d)$ has the interpretation that an individual chooses alternative x when faced with generalized choice situation $G = (X,d)$. A choice reversal, indicating preference incoherence under neoclassical assumptions, would be observed if $C(X,d_1) \neq C(X,d_2)$ for the different ancillary conditions d_1 and d_2.

The welfare analysis developed by Bernheim and Rangel identifies when observed choices allow for an assessment that one alternative is an improvement over another alternative because it is consistently chosen by the individual. In other words, when can one say that, based on the choice process being used by the individual, a policy change improves his or her welfare? To do so, they propose replacing the revealed preference axioms of neoclassical economics with axioms that restrict revealed preference to situations in which observed choices unambiguously indicate improvement. Rather than provide a full and rigorous exposition of their approach, which is best obtained from the original articles, the following avoids technical notation and presents only the strict preference relation to convey the essence of the approach.

The standard rational choice axioms include the relationship of strict preference, which indicates when an individual prefers x to y, written xPy: whenever the individual is faced with a choice situation involving x and y, the individual chooses x and never chooses y. The replacement for P, P*, indicates when an alternative x is strictly unambiguously chosen over y: xP^*y means that for all possible generalized choice situation (X,d) in which x and y are alternatives in X, the individual never chooses y. P* respects choices as revealing preference because it only applies when the choices are consistent; when choices are inconsistent, it does not apply: "In short, if there is a preference rationalization for choice, our framework employs that rationalization to evaluate welfare; when such a rationalization does not exist, our framework employs the most discerning relation that does not second-guess and overrule informed choice" (Bernheim 2009, 301). Thus, when it holds, it unambiguously supports the normative conclusion that x improves upon y. When choice does not depend on d, and the other axioms of choice hold, P* is equivalent to P so that the framework reverts to neoclassical welfare economics.

As should be expected in view of the possibility that P* does not hold for pairs of alternatives, the framework does not lead to a unique value of compensating variation for policy changes. Instead, it leads to two measures of compensating variation that define a region in which it is not clear if compensation for the policy change is adequate. Again, grossly simplifying notation, the two measures of compensating variation, m^A and m^B, can be written as follows for a change in environmental conditions from α_0 to α_1 with an accompanying change in ancillary conditions from d_0 to d_1 and a change in compensation from o to m:

$$yP^*x \text{ if } m \geq m^A \qquad\qquad \text{(EQ. 3.1)}$$

$$xP^*y \text{ if } m \leq m^B \qquad\qquad \text{(EQ. 3.2)}$$

where $x \in C(X(\alpha_0, o), d_0)$ and $y \in C(X(\alpha_1, m), d_1)$. The interpretation of these equations is that the new set of conditions (α_1, m, d_1) will be unambiguously chosen over the initial set of conditions (α_0, o, d_0) only if $m \geq m^A$ and $m \leq m^B$. As it can be shown that $m^A \geq m^B$, there are levels of compensation where the choice would be ambiguous and, therefore, so too would be whether or not the new conditions are an improvement.

Figure 3.1 illustrates the two measures of compensating variation. As in the example displayed in Figure 2.3, imagine a policy that allowed

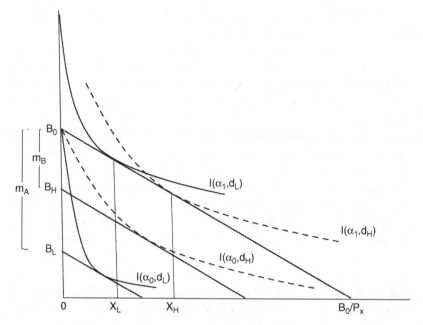

FIGURE 3.1 Compensating Variation in the Presence of Ancillary Conditions

the introduction of a market that will supply previously unavailable good X at price P_x. Before the introduction of the market, the consumer can only spend her budget, B_o, on goods other than X. However, depending on the way information about the good is presented to her, she has either indifference curve $I(\alpha_o, d_H)$ or indifference curve $I(\alpha_o, d_L)$. After introduction to the market, her highest obtainable indifference curves become $I(\alpha_1, d_H)$ or indifference curve $I(\alpha_1, d_L)$, and she will move from point (o, B_o) to point $(X_L, B_o - P_xX_L)$ if the ancillary condition has value d_L, and to point $(X_H, B_o - P_xX_H)$ if the ancillary condition has value d_H. The post-policy budgets to return the consumer to her original level of utility would be B_L and B_H, respectively, for conditions d_L and d_H. The compensating variations are thus $m_A = B_o - B_L$ and $m_B = B_o - B_H$. Because the analyst does not know which ancillary condition would apply if the policy were adopted, the compensating variation can only be bounded by the range from m_B to m_A. The same range would apply if the ancillary condition took on continuous values that position indifference curves between $I(\alpha_o, d_H)$ and $I(\alpha_o, d_L)$.

Note that the analysis in Figure 3.1 is possible because it assumed utility maximization conditional on the value of the ancillary condition—different positive models of choice would require different analyses. Also note that, as the difference between $I(\alpha_o, d_H)$ and $I(\alpha_o, d_L)$ declines, the less is the ambiguity in compensating variation. When the ancillary condition has little effect on utility, the range of compensating variation will be small and close to the compensating variation measured in the neoclassical framework. Finally, note that the measures of compensating variation for separate dimensions of policy changes cannot necessarily be summed to obtain cumulative bounds for compensating variation. Rather, the measures must be applied to a single policy change that incorporates all the dimensions of change.

Much of the technical heavy lifting in the choice framework involves defining generalized Pareto optimum based on P^*, defining a behavioral competitive equilibrium (sets of prices and ancillary conditions that clear all markets), and showing the conditions under which an allocation in a behavioral competitive equilibrium is a generalized Pareto optimum and therefore efficient. It had previously been shown that the competitive equilibrium in an exchange economy where consumers have incomplete or intransitive preferences is a Pareto optimum (Fon and Otani 1979). The framework generalizes the result both to positive choice models other than utility maximization and to economies with production.

The primary assumption needed for the behavioral competitive equilibrium to be a weak generalized Pareto optimum is that all choices confronted by individuals are welfare relevant in the sense that they potentially convey information about whether or not one alternative improves over another. If some of the possible choice situations were defined as not being welfare relevant, then this welfare theorem does not hold and it may be possible to find reallocations that increase the efficiency of the behavioral competitive equilibrium. Researchers may develop sufficient evidence to rule out certain choice situations as not welfare relevant: "The most promising possibility is to seek evidence that particular choices involve errors in processing factual information; we propose classifying those choices as 'mistakes' and excluding them from consideration" (Bernheim 2009, 293). For example, imagine that research showed that individuals had coherent preferences when faced with choice situations involving small numbers of alternatives, but either picked randomly or according to presentation order when faced with choice situations involving many alternatives. Analysts might then decide it is appropriate for assessing welfare to exclude choices from the large choice sets in applying the preference relations to identify welfare improvements. If data from these choices were included, then the behavioral competitive equilibrium would not necessarily be efficient because it may be possible to find a reallocation that improves upon the equilibrium. In this way, the framework at least opens the door for analysts to view certain choice situations as market failures that create the possibility for public policy interventions increasing efficiency.

Additional theorems within the choice framework allow Bernheim and Rangel (2009, 81–82) to make the important claim "that the standard welfare framework must be approximately correct when behavioral anomalies are small." This claim can be interpreted in Figure 3.1 as the ancillary condition having a small effect so that the indifference curves for d_H and d_L would be very close to each other, and consequently the compensating variation bounds would be close to each other and to the compensating variation we would calculate if utility did not depend on the ancillary condition. Therefore, in practical CBA, where we inevitably have substantial amounts of uncertainty in our predictions of impacts, we can reasonably ignore small deviations of behavior from the predictions of positive neoclassical models and focus our analytical attention on the larger ones. Specifically, following Bernheim and Rangel:

PGL 3.2 *In assessing benefits, ignore departures from rationality that do not substantially affect observed behaviors.*

The assessment of substantial effects requires some judgment in weighing relative magnitudes of estimation errors and the uncertainty in benefits arising from different ancillary conditions.

In a subsequent article, Bernheim (2016) distinguishes between two steps in what he calls a unified approach to behavioral economics. In the first step, analysts identify a welfare-relevant domain that identifies observed decisions that merit "deference"—that is, the particular ancillary conditions that cannot be ruled out as mistakes. Two conditions characterize a mistake:

First, a mistaken choice is predicated on a characterization of the available options and the outcomes they imply that is inconsistent with the information available to the decision maker . . . [second] . . . there is some other option in the opportunity set that the decision maker would select over the mistakenly chosen one in settings where characterization failure does *not* occur.   (p. 48)

In the second step, welfare assessment is based on the choices made in the welfare-relevant domain. So, for example, in Figure 3.1 the range of compensating variations would be m_B to m_A if decisions made under d_L and d_H were not mistakes.

Some empirical leverage may be available when the institutional rules for choice are related to ancillary conditions (Shogren and Thunström 2016). If rules tend to activate different ancillary conditions, then the range of plausible rules may bound the range of relevant ancillary conditions. For example, markets offering repeated decisions may prime decision utilities that are close to experienced utilities, while one-shot choice decisions may not. Researchers may be able to identify plausible bounds for ancillary conditions by observing behaviors over a plausible range of rules. Being able to do so may be fortuitous in observational studies, but potentially designed intentionally in experimental and stated preference studies. This line of argument, sketched by Shogren and Thunström (2016), suggests the following guideline:

PGL 3.3 *Take advantage of variation in institutional decision rules to help identify relevant ancillary conditions and the range of benefits that they imply.*

CONCLUSION

Economists have not ignored the problems that behavioral economics poses for neoclassical welfare economics. At one extreme, the distinction between decision and experienced utility provides an incremental approach of narrow scope that nonetheless has potential for practical application. At the other extreme, the opportunity criterion offers a radical approach of broad scope that unfortunately has little potential for practical application. It would certainly be intellectually satisfying to have a widely accepted unified behavioral welfare economics to guide CBA. The generalized choice framework comes closest to playing that role, but it does not provide much of the practical guidance actually needed to do CBA. Instead, keeping in mind the purpose of CBA—providing assessments of the relative efficiency of public policy alternatives—the approach taken in the next four chapters to address specific behavioral problems draws opportunistically on the ideas presented in this chapter. In view of the cascade of expediencies in moving from neoclassical welfare economics to practical CBA, such opportunism should not be shocking.

4

Risk Perception and Expected Utility Deviations

Life abounds with uncertainties. The consequences of the choices we make when faced with uncertainties range from the mundane, such as staying dry on a rainy day, to the personally salient, such as surviving an automobile accident, to the socially profound, such as avoiding a substantial rise in the sea level. Many public policies seek to inform us about uncertainties so we can make better choices; others seek to shape the nature of the uncertainties themselves to make it more likely we will avoid undesirable consequences or obtain desirable ones. Assessing the relative efficiency of these policies requires a simplification of the relevant uncertainty to a situation of *risk* characterized by a plausible prospect, or lottery, identifying possible, or at least analytically representative, outcomes (contingencies) and assigning probabilities to their realizations. The neoclassical welfare perspective assumes individuals act rationally in the face of risks to reveal their preferences, thereby providing a basis for valuation. However, much accumulated evidence suggests that individuals often make choices when faced with risks that do not appear fully rational, complicating prediction of their choices and bringing into question valuations predicated on rationality.

Prospect theory, the most prominent behavioral alternative to the expected utility hypothesis, provides a useful framework for organizing our consideration of people's difficulty in assessing risks (violations of BERA4 and BERA6) and their often apparent failure to make choices as if they were maximizing expected utility (violations of BERA1, BERA2, and BERA5). Circumstances in which prospect theory provides a better predictive model than expected utility theory pose challenges to neoclassical CBA in two ways: first, it brings into question the calculation of expected net benefits based on the weighting of valued outcomes with evidence-based probabilities; second, and more fundamentally, it raises concerns about both revealed and stated preferences as the bases for the valuation of outcomes. Prospect theory also provides a starting point for discussion in the next chapter of the wide discrepancies often observed between willingness to pay and willingness to accept (potential violation of BERA3).

PROSPECT THEORY AS BEHAVIORAL ORGANIZING PRINCIPLE

Not long after John von Neumann and Oskar Morgenstern (1944) introduced expected utility theory, Maurice Allais (1953) presented a situation in which people seemed to make choices inconsistent with it. As part of his refutation of the "American school" adoption of Bernoulli-type (von Neumann and Morgenstern) expected utility, he presented two pairs of lotteries constructed in such a way that, under the expected utility hypothesis, the choice of one lottery in the first pair was only consistent with the choice of one of the lotteries in the second pair. However, many people confronted with the lottery pairs make inconsistent choices.

Experimental evidence showing behavior inconsistent with the expected utility hypothesis accumulated (Starmer 2000). For example, experiments showed possible reversals in preferences based on the mode of choice presented to subjects. Sarah Lichtenstein and Paul Slovic (1971) constructed pairs of lotteries with the same expected value, but with one lottery having a high probability of the positive payoff (the so-called P-bet) and the other with a larger magnitude of positive payoff (the so-called $-bet). Subjects often selected the P-bet but placed a higher valuation (that is, expressed a larger willingness to pay) for the $-bet, thus showing an inconsistency. Indeed, such a preference reversal would potentially make the individual a "money pump," whose assets could be drained without risk by an unscrupulous agent selling a $-bet to the individual at the higher price, trading it with the individual for the P-bet, and buying the P-bet back at the lower price, and so forth (Smith 1985). Similarly, a mode effect commonly appears in elicitations of utilities—varying the probabilities of a lottery to find indifference between a stated certain payment and the lottery (probability equivalence method) often results in a lottery that would require a larger certain payment for indifference if it were determined by varying the size of the certain payment (certainty equivalence method), a result clearly inconsistent with the expected utility hypothesis (Hershey and Schoemaker 1985). Such dependence on the mode of choice has led some to make the more general argument that preferences themselves are labile and often inconsistent (Lichtenstein and Slovic 2006).

Drawing on their own experimental work, as well as the accumulating experimental evidence from other behavioral researchers, Daniel Kahneman and Amos Tversky (1979) challenged the expected utility hypothesis as a descriptive, and implicitly predictive, model of choice and proposed an alternative that they called "prospect theory." Building on several conceptual innovations (including those of Quiggin 1982, Yaari 1987, and Schmeidler 1989), they subsequently revised the theory to accommodate multiple outcomes, to impose restrictions on the cumulative distribution of decision weights (hence the name "cumulative prospect theory"), and to allow for its application to situations of uncertainty as well as risk (Tversky and Kahneman 1992). Prospect theory has been further developed to allow for uncertain reference points (Schmidt et al. 2008). A somewhat stylized version of prospect theory follows.

We begin with a prospect, which we call alternative A: possible wealth outcomes $S_1, S_2, \ldots, S_K$ ordered from smallest to largest with respective probabilities $p_1, p_2, \ldots, p_K$. For the time being, consider these probabilities to be "objective" in the sense of being based on either logical analysis of relative frequencies or scientifically sound empirical evidence. Prospect theory allows individuals to have decision weights, $w_k(p_k)$, that may depend on the objective probabilities. Cumulative prospect theory constructs decision weights for the ordered outcomes so that they are all positive and sum to one. These rank-dependent decision weights allow for the introduction of pessimism, the overweighting of the probabilities of extremely negative outcomes, and optimism, the overweighting of extremely positive outcomes, as well as other deviations from objective probabilities while preserving the properties of a proper cumulative probability distribution (Cartwright 2011).

Rather than valuing outcome S_k in terms of a utility function, $U(S_k)$, that depends only on wealth in the realized outcome, prospect theory introduces a valuation function that depends on the change in wealth from some reference point. In the simplest version, the valuation function depends on changes in wealth. If the initial wealth is S_o, then the function depends on the difference, $S_k - S_o$. The valuation function itself may differ depending on the sign of this difference. In more complicated versions of prospect theory, the reference point may differ from current wealth or be randomly determined, perhaps by the circumstances of choice.

As a specific example, consider the following valuation function, which has the basic shape of the one proposed by Tversky and Kahneman (1992):

$$v(S_k) = \begin{cases} [(S_k - S_o)/1000]^\alpha & \text{if } S_k \geq S_o \\ -\lambda [(S_o - S_k)/1000]^\beta & \text{if } S_k < S_o \end{cases} \qquad \text{(EQ. 4.1)}$$

where α, β, and λ are positive-valued parameters that determine the shape of the valuation function for outcome S_k relative to a reference point S_o. Note the asymmetry between gains ($S_k > S_o$) and losses ($S_k < S_o$). Figure 4.1 displays $v(S_k)$ for values of S_k between \$100 thousand and \$0 relative to a reference wealth of S_o equal to \$50 thousand for $\alpha = 0.5$, $\beta = 0.6$, and $\lambda = 1.5$. These parameter values produce a typical prospect valuation function that places more weight on losses than on comparable gains. For example, in Figure 4.1, a gain of \$20 thousand in wealth would be valued at about positive 4.5 while a loss of \$20 thousand would be valued at about minus 9.0; the difference in the valuation function of going from the loss to the gain would be 13.5, or a gain of about 150 percent in moving from the loss to the gain. In contrast, consider a utility function

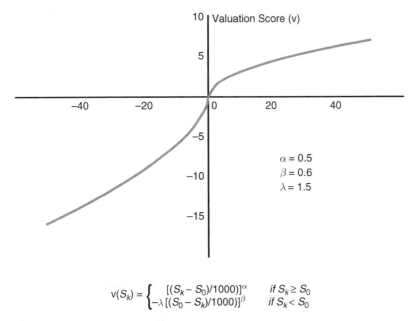

$$v(S_k) = \begin{cases} [(S_k - S_0)/1000]^\alpha & \text{if } S_k \geq S_0 \\ -\lambda [(S_0 - S_k)/1000]^\beta & \text{if } S_k < S_0 \end{cases}$$

FIGURE 4.1 Typical Prospect Theory Valuation Function

that weighted outcomes in a way similar to this valuation function for gains, $(S_k/1000)^\alpha$ where $\alpha = 0.5$. It would give a utility of 5.5 for $30 thousand ($50 thousand minus $20 thousand) and 8.4 for $70 thousand ($50 thousand plus $20 thousand), or an increase in the utility of the gain of only about 53 percent, a much smaller difference than that of the valuation function.

Putting the decision weights and outcome valuation function together gives the following expression:

$$V_A = \sum_{k=1}^{K} w_k(p_k)v(S_k) \qquad \text{(EQ. 4.2)}$$

where V_A is the valuation of prospect A. If the person is choosing between two prospects, A and B, then prospect theory predicts that the person will choose A over B if $V_A > V_B$, choose B over A if $V_A < V_B$, and be indifferent between A and B if $V_A = V_B$. For the ranking of alternatives according to this valuation function to be fully consistent with rankings in terms of expected utility, the decision weights must be linear in probabilities: that is, $w_k(p_k) = p_k$. In other words, the individual must use objective probabilities as decision weights in Equation 4.2. For the differences in valuations of the alternatives to correspond to those from expected utility, the reference outcome must be set to zero so that valuation depends on outcomes rather than on gains and losses. When these conditions do not hold, policies shown to be efficient under the assumption that individuals are maximizing expected utility may not be efficient. For example, the conventional principles of optimal taxation do not hold if prospect theory describes individual choices under uncertainty (Kanbur et al. 2008).

The primary focus of this chapter is on deviations of decision weights from objective probabilities; the primary focus of the next chapter is on the implications of non-zero reference outcomes in the interpretation of large differences between willingness to pay and willingness to accept.

SYSTEMATIC BIASES IN SUBJECTIVE PROBABILITIES

Although the laws of probability seem simple once learned, their discovery, driven considerably by desires to win games of chance, required the best minds of the Enlightenment and, for many students in introductory courses in probability and statistics, learning them does not always come easily. Indeed, consider a recent international survey of people aged 16 to 65 years that assessed their numeracy in terms of five levels of proficiency, with levels 4 and 5 including an understanding of chance. Only 8 percent of US respondents were able to do tasks showing these levels of proficiency (Goodman et al. 2013). Of course, those who didn't achieve at least level 4 might actually be able to use probabilities in tasks but may fall short on other aspects of numeracy. Nonetheless, a large body of experimental research suggests that many people do have difficulty estimating probabilities and manipulating them according to the laws of probability.

Tversky and Kahneman (1974) argued that people used generally useful heuristics to simplify complex tasks that nonetheless can lead to large systematic errors, or biases. They identified three heuristics and explained how the use of each could lead to bias. First, in assessing the probability that some object belongs in some larger class of objects, people often employ the representativeness heuristic: their probabilities reflect the degree to which the object is representative of the objects in the class. For example, given the description of a male as large, young, and athletic, people might very well assess the probability of the person being a professional football player as more than trivially larger than zero. If the described person were randomly selected from the population, then even a probability estimate of only a few percent would be much too large because the frequency of professional football players in the population is extremely small. Such a bias arises because people tend to be insensitive to prior probabilities, or underlying frequencies, in their assessments using the representativeness heuristic. Biases can also arise in using the representativeness heuristic a number of other ways, including insensitivity to sample size, overconfidence in prediction when the object fits the class well, and unawareness of regression toward the mean—all factors that may contribute to a general overconfidence in the prediction of uncertain events (Malmendier and Taylor 2015). People also often have a misunderstanding of the law of large numbers (for example, after three heads in a row, a head on the next flip of a fair coin is less likely than a tail—the invalid "law of small numbers" that seems to motivate many gamblers who believe a tail is due).

Second, in assessing probabilities as frequencies of occurrences, people often employ the availability heuristic: their probabilities reflect the ease with which occurrences can be brought to mind. For example, knowing someone who recently suffered a house fire or regularly watching local news programs that cover house fires will likely lead one to make a higher estimate of the frequency of house fires than would be the case without such sources of easy recall. This heuristic can lead to biases because many extraneous factors affect one's ability to retrieve instances, such as their saliency when they became memories and how recently they occurred. Biases can also arise because individuals do not always search for instances systematically, because they often have difficulty in imagining instances not available in memory, and because they sometimes estimate probabilities using an incorrect linking of events based on illusory correlations.

Third, in incorporating new information into estimates of probabilities, people often follow the adjustment and anchoring heuristic: probabilities are derived from adjustments to initial values based on the formulation of the problem or partial calculation. Biases arise because people tend to make insufficient adjustments to initial estimates and experts asked to provide probability distributions tend to anchor them too narrowly around their point estimates. They also arise because anchoring tends to lead to overestimation of the probabilities of conjunctive events, such as a succession of successful events (the final probability tends to be anchored by the probability of the first event, which is necessarily larger than the overall probability), and to underestimation of the probabilities of disjunctive events, such as any successful event from among a set of events (the final probability tends to be anchored by the probability of first event considered, which is necessarily smaller than the overall probability).

A sort of anchoring also operates in the processing of information relevant to the assessment of risks (Slovic 1987), which combines probabilities with outcomes. Strongly held initial beliefs about risks tend to be resistant to change in the face of new evidence because the beliefs tend to influence the way individuals process it. New information contrary to the initial beliefs tends to be dismissed as erroneous or irrelevant. In addition to the perceived voluntariness of the risk—that is, the extent to which individuals can avoid it if they so choose—"other (perceived) characteristics such as familiarity, control, catastrophic potential, equity, and level of knowledge also seem to influence the relations between perceived risk, perceived benefit, and risk acceptance" (Slovic 1987, 283).

The biases that result from the heuristics individuals use to assess probabilities and risks depend greatly on particular applications and their circumstances. Nevertheless, a few generalizations stand out: Individuals tend to underestimate large probabilities (Lichtenstein et al. 1978) and appear to be make one of two very different errors in estimating small probabilities, either overestimating them or ignoring them completely (Camerer and Kunreuther 1989; McClelland et al. 1993; Reyna 2004). The misperception of small probabilities is particularly important for two reasons. First, many public policies addressing health, safety, and environmental issues involve risks with small probabilities. Second, many valuations based on revealed preferences involve observing tradeoffs between things of value, such as wealth or time, and small differences in mortality risk.

These deviations of subjective probabilities from evidence-based probabilities, as well as several of the other anomalies that motivate prospect theory, can be explained by an adjustment to expected utility that Viscusi (1989) calls "prospective reference theory." It assumes that people assess evidence-based estimates of probabilities provided to them using a Bayesian-like process in which they treat the evidence-based estimates as imperfect in their updating of their prior, or reference (initial subjective) probabilities. When reference probabilities are equal across outcomes, they will tend to anchor the resulting updated subjective probabilities away from the extremes, producing the overestimation of small probabilities and the underestimation of large probabilities.

It has also long been observed that people show an aversion to ambiguity about probabilities (Ellsberg 1961). For example, when told only that an urn contains red and black balls, most people would be equally willing to bet on red or black as the outcome of a draw. Similarly, most people are equally likely to bet on a red draw as a black draw when they are told that an urn contains exactly 50 red and 50 black balls. However, if given the choice between betting on, say, a red draw from the urn with an unknown distribution of colors and a red draw from an urn with equal numbers of red and black balls, most people show a preference for the second bet. In other words, although they apparently subjectively assess the probability of drawing a red ball as ½ in the case in which they do not know the distribution, they nonetheless prefer the bet involving a draw from the urn in which they know the frequency of red to be ½.

Much of the evidence challenging the expected utility hypothesis comes from laboratory experiments. On the one hand, these experiments have great internal validity because they allow for selective variation of treatments in controlled circumstances, typically with random assignment to treatment groups. On the other hand, one can question the external validity of these experiments with respect to the sorts of behaviors relevant to public policy. Most importantly, for practical reasons, the experiments typically involve relatively small payoffs that may not make outcomes sufficiently salient to elicit full use of cognitive resources. Also, many of the experiments involve college students as subjects, a sample not necessarily relevant to the general population, especially in light of the growing evidence that adolescence and its behaviors extend into the mid-20s (Johnson et al. 2009). However, buttressing the experimental evidence, apparent violations of expected utility appear to occur in the "wild" as well. Colin Camerer (2004) identified findings from observational research in finance, labor, consumer choice, insurance, and gambling that appear more consistent with prospect than expected utility theory.

The following sections consider three ways that misperceived probabilities may be relevant to CBA: first, in the calculation of expected surpluses; second, in the use of specific benefit estimates and more general shadow prices from studies using revealed preference methods; and third, in the use of stated preference methods to elicit option prices.

APPROPRIATE PROBABILITIES FOR CALCULATING EXPECTED SURPLUS

Many public policies involve the expenditure of real resources to obtain reductions in risks borne by individuals. For example, restrictions on the use of a particular pesticide may require farmers to purchase protective gear for their employees and train them in how to use it properly so as to reduce the employees' probabilities of developing a specific cancer. Assessing the efficiency of this policy through CBA would require analysts to confront uncertainty about the various parameters they would employ in predicting costs and benefits: unit costs of equipment, quantity of equipment, useful life of equipment, cost of training, quantity of training and retraining, cost of enforcement, costs of the pesticide and any substitutes, avoided risk of cancer from reduced exposure, treatment and quality of life costs for cancer, and the value of avoided mortalities, among others. As these sorts of *parameter uncertainties* are ubiquitous in CBA, good practice typically involves using Monte Carlo simulations to take account of them in producing a predicted distribution of net benefits rather than a single estimate or a small number of alternative estimates resulting from selectively changing assumed parameter values (Vining and Weimer 2010; Weimer 2015). Not taking account of parameter uncertainties and the uncertainty they induce in net benefit predictions is akin to reporting statistical estimates without standard errors.

Risk reduction policies also involve what can be called *analytical risks*—the characterization of policies' impacts in terms of changes in the prospects individuals face. In the pesticide example, the policy would change the probabilities of cancer faced by workers. So, for example, a policy that was fully effective in eliminating exposure to the pesticide might change the risk of developing the particular cancer from some small probability to nearly zero. The behavioral problem for CBA arises when individuals' subjective estimates of the risks differ from those based on the available scientific evidence.

Predictions of the benefit of the prospect improvement provided by a policy to a person would ideally answer the question: What is the largest payment that the person would be willing to make to obtain the prospect improvement before knowing which contingency actually results? This ex-ante (before contingencies are realized) payment is the person's option price (Graham 1981). Summing such payments across all individuals would provide a measure of aggregate benefit. It would be certain in the sense that it would not depend on which contingency actually occurred. It would be preference-based, and incorporate people's subjective probabilities, which could be informed with evidence-based estimates. Considering only analytical risk (that is, ignoring parameter uncertainty), the sum of the option prices would be a riskless benefit measure that could be compared to a riskless cost, providing a riskless prediction of net benefits. In most situations of analytical risk, option price, which is fully reflective of preferences over risky alternatives, is the proper metric for predicting benefits (Boardman et al. 2011).

Estimates of option prices can be obtained through stated preference methods. However, high cost as well as inherent challenges in their design and to their expeditious implementation often make contingent valuation and other stated preference surveys either impractical or an inefficient use of analytical resources for those conducting CBAs. The common expediency is to predict the benefits of prospect changes by assessing the consumer surplus to the individual in each contingency and then weighting these surpluses with their respective probabilities of the contingencies. The resulting benefits are labeled "ex post" in that they are based on people's valuation of contingencies as if they have occurred. The ex-post assessment of welfare was originally justified by the extension of the neoclassical welfare theorems to include risk through the definition of contingencies as separate goods that can be traded (Arrow 1964). However, critics noted a number of ways that ex-post and ex-ante assessments differed (Harris and Olewiler 1979; Hammond 1981; Sandmo 1983), raising questions about whether ex-post efficiency is the proper welfare criterion.

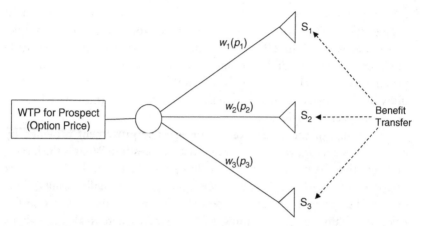

Expected Surplus (Evidence-Based Probabilities): $ES_e = p_1S_1 + p_2S_2 + p_3S_3$

Expected Surplus (Subjective Probabilities): $ES_s = w_1(p_1)S_1 + w_2(p_2)S_2 + w_3(p_3)S_3$

FIGURE 4.2 Ex-Ante and Ex-Post Willingness to Pay for a Prospect

Figure 4.2 illustrates the difference between option price and expected surplus for a prospect with three possible outcomes occurring with evidence-based probabilities p_1, p_2, and p_3. The option price is the most the person would be willing to pay for the prospect before the actual contingency is revealed. The standard expected surplus, ES_e, is the sum of the person's willingness to pay for each of the contingencies (S_1, S_2, and S_3) weighted by their respective evidence-based probabilities. However, from the perspective of the person, the probabilities to use in calculating the expected surplus would be $w_1(p_1)$, $w_2(p_2)$, and $w_3(p_3)$ resulting in ES_s.

In general, option price and expected surplus differ. The difference defines option value: if option price exceeds expected surplus, then option value is positive; if expected surplus exceeds option price, then option value is negative. When the concept of option value was originally introduced, some environmental economists argued that it would always be positive, and therefore always an excluded positive benefit in CBAs based on expected surplus (Cicchetti and Freeman 1971). Subsequent analysis, however, showed that option value need not be positive (Schmalensee 1972) and depended on the nature of demand and whether the policy change affected the prices, quantities, or qualities of goods (Larson and Flacco 1992). In general, risk-averse individuals will have positive option values for policies that reduce income risk.

Admittedly, if the risky outcomes are independent across individuals, such as the risk posed by a carcinogen or a stretch of highway prone to accident, and there is a large number of individuals exposed to the risk, then the predicted ex-post benefit will be approximately certain by the law of large numbers, and therefore approximately commensurate with certain costs. However, although effectively certain, these benefits based on expected surplus do not correspond to the correct social valuation, which is the sum of individuals' option prices, In contrast, if the risky outcomes are not independent, such as extremely so in the case of social risks like earthquakes or nuclear accidents, then the predicted ex-post benefit will be highly uncertain as well as incorrect. Thus, in neither case does the use of expected surplus to predict benefits fully take account of individual preferences.

Nonetheless, the vast majority of CBAs done by analysts in government agencies predict benefits in terms of expected surpluses rather than option prices. Reductions in mortality risk are monetized by multiplying them by the willingness of individuals to pay for them. Sometimes the risk reductions can be identified for groups differentiated by characteristics such as income or age and estimates of average willingness to pay for each group applied to the sum of mortality reductions for that group. Often monetization takes the shortcut of aggregating reductions in mortality risks to predict the number of avoided deaths, which is then multiplied by a shadow price for the value of a life. The expediency of using expected surplus rather than option price as the basis for measuring benefits of risk reductions suggests the following guideline:

PGL 4.1 *Use evidence-based probabilities in expected surplus analyses even when there is reason to believe that they differ from subjective probabilities.*

The primary argument supporting PGL 4.1 recognizes the distinction between decision and experienced utility introduced in Chapter 3. Using evidence-based probabilities can be thought of as consistent with maximizing experienced utility. If we accept empirically estimated statistical values of contingent surpluses as valid, then evidence-based probabilities better capture the value of the risk changes to consumers than does the use of their subjective probabilities. As noted, however, using evidence-based probabilities with contingent surpluses only approximates the benefits that would be predicted for risk changes based on the option prices of individuals whose subjective probabilities were evidence based.

INTERPRETATION OF BENEFIT TRANSFERS BASED ON REVEALED PREFERENCES

The use of expected surpluses potentially suffers from a divergence between subjective and evidence-based probabilities in the process of "benefit transfer," the use of estimates from existing studies to predict contingent benefits, such as S_1, S_2, and S_3 in Figure 4.2. Benefit transfer ranges from the use of a context-specific estimate of a benefit taken from a single study to a generic shadow price based on numerous studies. Almost all of practical CBA involves benefit transfer—direct estimation is only possible if benefits can be estimated by applying revealed preference methods to data arising from an existing policy to predict that policy's future benefits or if benefits can be obtained from stated preferences methods applied in surveys asking explicitly about a proposed policy. Indeed, the term originated in the use of CBA in environmental policy where stated preference methods sometimes can be used as the basis for predicting the benefits of specific policies.

As an example of a generic shadow price, consider the extremely important estimate of the value of statistical life—perhaps more accurately, and less provocatively, it should be called "willingness to swap (WTS) alternative goods and services for a microrisk reduction in the chance of sudden death" (Cameron 2010, 161)—"swap" conveys that people do trade things like time or convenience (as well as money) for changes in mortality risk and "microrisk" emphasizes that valuation is based on how people trade small risk reductions. It can be argued that simply referring to the value of mortality reductions rather than the value of statistical life would be a more accurate and less provocative term than statistical value of life (US Environmental Protection Agency 2010).

Revealed preference studies estimate the implicit value people put on their own lives by the way they trade money or time for small changes in mortality risk. (For reviews, see Viscusi and Aldy 2003; Viscusi 2013, 2015a; Cropper et al. 2011; and Robinson and Hammitt 2016.) The most common tradeoff considered is between wages and occupational mortality risk. Hedonic regressions allow the premiums demanded for accepting riskier jobs to be separated from the premiums for other relevant job characteristics such as injury risk. Controlling for these other job characteristics and assuming individuals make decisions based on expected utility, annual wages that are $1,000 higher for a job with a 1 in 10,000 higher chance of annual mortality is consistent with the marginal worker making decisions as if he or she is valuing his or her life at $10 million ($1,000/0.0001).

Two potential problems arise if people misperceive probabilities. First, random deviations of perceived probabilities from the evidence-based probabilities used in the statistical analyses would tend to bias estimates toward zero because of the errors-in-variables problem. The impact of errors in mortality risk data was dramatically demonstrated by a doubling of the estimate of the value of statistical life resulting from the availability of more accurate US job mortality data in 1987 (Moore and Viscusi 1988). Limiting consideration of US labor market studies to those that use data from after 1992 when the Bureau of Labor Statistics introduced the Census of Fatal Occupational Injuries provides more accurate estimates (US Environmental Protection Agency 2010; US Department of Transportation 2014b; Robinson and Hammitt 2015).

Second, systematic error in perceived probabilities could also bias estimates. Annual occupational mortality risks are relatively small. Imagine that, consistent with the risk perception literature, people generally overestimate these risks. For instance, instead of the marginal employee perceiving the evidence-based extra mortality risk as 1 in 10,000 as in the previous example, assume that he or she perceived it as 2 in 10,000. In other words, the person is demanding the $1,000 wage premium for a larger probability of mortality than assumed by the observer relying on the evidence-based probability. This misperception would lead to an estimate of the statistical value of life of $5 million rather than $10 million. Interestingly, stated preference studies in which people are presented with probabilities tend to find somewhat smaller statistical values of life (Lindhjem et al. 2011; Robinson and Hammitt 2016).

Much of the empirical research testing the expected utility hypothesis implicitly assumes that those generating the data are homogenous in the sense that they all are following the same decision model. However, in many situations it is possible that different people use different decision processes, perhaps depending on the saliency of the decision to them personally and their experience in confronting similar decisions. Ignoring this heterogeneity by assuming that all people follow the same model leads to a specification error for at least some of the data. Harrison and Rutström (2009) demonstrate the implications of decision-model heterogeneity by using a mixture model that simultaneously estimates the parameters of expected utility and prospect theory specifications as well as the probabilities of individual subjects employing each of the decision processes. In their particular lottery experiment, approximately equal numbers of subjects appeared to be making choices according to the expected utility and prospect theory specifications. Assuming that all participants were making decisions according to prospect theory resulted in estimates of parameters only weakly consistent with a priori expectations; however, allowing for heterogeneity through estimation of the mixture model resulted in estimates of the parameters that were "strikingly consistent" with prospect theory (p.146). Further, they showed that some of the heterogeneity in the decision process could be explained by demographic characteristics, with women, African American, and Hispanic participants more likely to make decisions as if they are following prospect rather than expected utility theory.

Revealed preference methods employed outside of the laboratory typically focus on aggregate outcomes that arise from a population interacting within markets or other institutions—estimates of the wage premiums in labor markets for bearing greater mortality or injury risk, differences in property values in residential real estate markets resulting from location-specific ambient noise levels or other local amenities or disamenities, or differences in visits to scenic venues as a function of variation in travel costs. How sensitive are these aggregate outcomes to populations that are heterogeneous with respect to decision processes? Do some institutions tend to encourage the dominance of expected utility maximization through participation incentives or learning? Are some institutions less sensitive to alternative decision processes? In other words, should we expect to see some institutions revealing preferences consistent with the expected utility hypothesis even when a substantial number of participants do not seem to be following it in their individual choices?

As already noted, the review of observational studies by Camerer (2004) found a number of situations in which market behavior did not appear consistent with the expected utility hypothesis, suggesting at least that institutional mitigation is not always complete. In an earlier article, Camerer (1987) identified six arguments advanced by economists for why markets might produce rational results even if some of the participants were irrational. First, in many markets, individuals have sufficient financial incentive and experience to avoid mistakes. Second, markets will tend to cancel out the mistakes of individual participants. Third, a small number of rational participants may be enough to produce rational market outcomes if they have sufficient access to capital so that their actions dominate the market. Fourth, less rational participants may learn from more experienced participants (implicit learning). Fifth, less rational participants may buy advice from more experienced participants (explicit learning). And sixth, less rational participants may suffer losses that drive them from markets.

An experimental literature finds support for several of these arguments for specific types of markets. Camerer (1987) conducted an experiment to assess whether prices and allocations approached those consistent with Bayesian updating in a series of double-oral auctions in which participants publically made offers to buy or sell assets. Except in cases in which the new information was extreme, prices and allocations approached those consistent with Bayesian updating. Cox and Grether (1996) designed an experiment to see if preference reversals over bet pairs decline in repeated second-price sealed bid auctions. Although telltale asymmetric preference reversals were present in the initial rounds of the experiment, they were eliminated by the fifth round in versions of the experiments that provided subjects with financial incentives. In an experiment simulating investment banking in which informed agents must infer the predictions of less informed agents, Camerer et al. (1989) found that participation in a double-oral auction reduced the magnitude of the "knowledge curse": the inability of better informed participants to ignore their own private information when predicting the behavior of less informed participants, but only by about 50 percent relative to their individual assessments. Evans (1997) constructed an experiment using a fifth-price auction in which groups of subjects submitted sealed bids for lotteries, with the four highest bidders allowed to purchase at the fifth highest bid, so that the bidders have an incentive to bid their highest values. The auction prices showed much lower rates of violation of the expected utility hypothesis than the rates observed at the individual level, primarily by eliminating the influence of extreme bids.

These experiments assess the role of particular market institutions in mitigating individual deviations from the expected utility hypothesis. Not all market institutions will necessarily do so. For example, common value auctions, in which bidders with different information will receive the same, ex-post value from an offered asset, such as an oil concession, have long been known to be vulnerable to the "winner's curse," in which the bidder who happens to have the largest positive error in the estimation of value will win but either suffer a net loss or make less profit than anticipated. Rational bidders should anticipate this statistical phenomenon and reduce their bids accordingly to avoid the curse (Cox and Isaac 1984). Nonetheless, both experimental and observational evidence suggest that the winner's curse usually occurs in common value auctions (Thaler 1988).

In using the results of empirical research in any type of policy analysis, one should be concerned about internal validity, the likelihood that claimed causal relationships actually exist within the sampled population, and external validity, the likelihood that the claimed relationships apply to a different population. Laboratory experiments using random assignment of subjects to control groups generally have high levels of internal validity, but they may have low levels of external validity for populations of interest. Observational studies using data from the population of interest may have low levels of internal validity, but high levels of external validity. Academic research tends to focus almost exclusively on internal validity; good policy analysis requires attention to both internal and external validity. Accepting some threat to internal validity to get substantial improvements in external validity may be appropriate.

Benefit transfer from existing studies for use in CBA also should consider what can be called *benefit validity*. That is, does individual irrationality threaten the validity of the neoclassical interpretation of findings in the prediction of benefits? It facilitates a "behavioral transfer test" (Viscusi and Gayer 2016). Our particular concern in this section arises from the findings of many laboratory experiments and some field research that individuals often make errors in formulating, updating, and applying probabilities in situations involving risk, leading to the following practical guideline:

PGL 4.2 *In benefit transfer from studies involving risk to expected surplus analyses, assess benefit validity by considering the likelihood that individuals irrationally estimate, update, or apply probabilities and the extent to which institutional arrangements mitigate irrationality with respect to the aggregates used in benefit prediction.*

As with PGL 4.1, this guideline accepts experienced utility as the proper basis for valuation. That is, individuals would be better off after the resolution of prospects if they did not make errors in using probabilities.

Unfortunately, we do not have an accepted taxonomy of benefit validity comparable to the systematic treatment provided by Campbell and Stanley (1963), and the many works that followed, of the internal validity of research designs. As with external validity, our approach to benefit validity must draw on what we know about various populations. In the case of benefit validity, it appears that saliency and familiarity are two relevant factors for anticipating individual irrationality, and that institutional arrangements fostering learning and mitigating extremes contribute to market rationality. So, for example, interpreting the winning bid for an unfamiliar prospect in a common value auction as a willingness to pay for the prospect is likely questionable; accepting the value of statistical life based on multiple studies of risk premiums in labor markets is much less so. From the perspective of CBA, a valuable project for behavioral economists would be the development of more systematic advice about how to assess benefit validity.

BENEFIT TRANSFERS AND ELICITED OPTION PRICES FROM STATED PREFERENCE STUDIES

Stated preference methods provide an opportunity to communicate probabilities directly to individuals. In some cases, the communication seeks to move respondents' probability weights, the $w_i(p_i)$ in Figure 4.2, closer to evidence-based probabilities. In other cases, such as the presentation of hypothetical risks to develop evidence relevant to benefit transfer, the communication seeks to get respondents to accept particular probabilities for unfamiliar risks. In either case, effective communication of the probabilities is an essential feature of research design.

Two types of guidance emerge from reviews of research on risk communication. First, some general recommendations seem well supported: the presentation should use the same denominator for all probabilities—frequencies, percentages, base rates, or proportions should not be mixed; and, because people often incorrectly interpret relative risk reductions as absolute risk reductions, the latter should be used to avoid confusion (Visschers et al. 2009).

Second, some recommendations about appropriate processes for implementing risk communication have been made: the numerical and risk literacy of respondents should be assessed and accommodated; risk presentation methods should be evaluated using validity tests, such as sensitivity to probability changes; and data should be collected to assess heterogeneity of respondents' knowledge and risk preferences (Harrison et al. 2014). Graphics, facilitated by on-line survey instruments, may be more effective than purely numeric presentations, but more research on the implications of specific formats is needed (Visschers et al. 2009; Harrison et al. 2014; Corso et al. 2001).

The growing literature on risk communication relevant to stated preference methods suggests the following guideline:

PGL 4.3 *The conduct of stated preference studies involving prospects should communicate probabilities using the best available guidance from the risk communication literature; the assessment of benefit validity in existing studies should consider compliance with risk communication guidance.*

Risk communication should be interpreted broadly to include efforts to help respondents better understand their own risk-related preferences. Specifically, interactive learning within survey instruments administered by computer can potentially reduce preference reversals. Cherry et al. (2003) demonstrate the possibility of "rationality spillovers" from market experience to the valuation of non-market goods. In a laboratory experiment, subjects made choices of lotteries from $-bet and P-bet pairs and valued them. One pair of lotteries represented market goods, such that lotteries were sold to the subject if stated values were larger than a randomly selected price. The other pair of lotteries represented non-market goods as chances of interacting with wildlife in Yellowstone National Park. In each of ten rounds following an initial five, an arbitrage treatment subjected those whose lottery choices and valuations showed preference reversals to an explained step-by-step implementation of a "money pump." The arbitrage treatment dramatically reduced the fraction of preference reversals in the traded goods from about 33 percent to about 5 percent by the last round. This result is consistent with this particular market institution reducing the incidence of preference reversals. More surprisingly, the arbitrage treatment also reduced the incidence of preference reversals in lotteries for the non-traded good. It thus appears that learning about the consequences of preference reversals in the simulated market reduced preference reversals with respect to the hypothetical good. Admittedly, the simulated market in this experiment was unusual in that it not just exploited participants, it also explained to them how they were being exploited. Nonetheless, the possibility of achieving rationality spillovers of this sort may eventually justify the extra effort they require in the design and implementation of stated preference studies (Hanley and Shogren 2005).

What should analysts do when stated preference studies with questionable risk communication protocols provide the only sources for benefit transfer? For example, the CBA of a health intervention may require use of a quality-adjusted life-year (QALY), an estimate of the utility of living with a disease symptom. (For an overview, see Robinson and Hammitt 2013.) The available estimate may come from a published cost-effectiveness study that conducted probability equivalence or time-tradeoff exercises with samples of patients or the public as barebones supplements to effectiveness assessment without much attention to risk communication. These methods assume that respondents are maximizing expected utility. If analysts suspect instead that the choices of respondents would be better described by prospect theory, then they may want to consider an adjustment to the reported utilities developed by Bleichrodt et al. (2001). It corrects for the resulting bias using empirical estimates of the parameters of the canonical model of prospect theory provided by Tversky and Kahneman (1992).

The contingent valuation method (CVM) survey has been the stated preference method most commonly used by economists to estimate willingness to pay; considerable guidance on the craft of CVM has accumulated (Freeman et al. 2014). CVM surveys provide a way of directly estimating option price by asking for a valuation of the sorts of prospects shown in Figure 4.2. A general challenge to the design of valid CVM surveys arises because the valuation is hypothetical. Respondents must have sufficient information to understand the good being valued (Blomquist and Whitehead 1998) and to respond as if they were making economic decisions that take account of their limited budgets (Carson and Groves 2007). Research into effective communication of risks has been part of the CVM project almost since its beginning (Jones-Lee et al. 1985; Smith and Desvousges 1987; Loomis and DuVair 1993). The increasing use of internet-based survey instruments has increased the feasibility of giving respondents much more, and more interactively presented, information, including various graphic formats (Corso et al. 2001), than can be provided through other survey modes (Berrens et al. 2004).

Two tests are now commonly used to assess the validity of willingness-to-pay estimates from CVM surveys (Carson et al. 2001). First, the results should demonstrate a negative own-price elasticity for the good being valued. In the context of the referendum format, which is now widely viewed as the preferred elicitation method, validity requires that the higher the randomly assigned "bid price," the smaller the fractions of respondents who accept it. A variety of design problems can produce too small a price response, including simply not providing adequate variation in the bid prices to produce meaningful differences in response rates. Avoiding these problems usually requires various sorts of pretests that also provide an opportunity to improve risk communication. (Note that a positive income elasticity of willingness to pay was originally considered by many researchers to be a comparable validity test to negative own-price elasticity, but is generally no longer applied because an increase in the quantity of a good purchased with respect to increases in income does not necessarily imply an increase in willingness to pay with respect increases in income [Flores and Carson 1997].)

Second, the results should pass a scope test with respect to the quantity or quality of the good being valued. Larger quantities or higher qualities of the good, other things equal, should elicit greater acceptance of bid prices and therefore larger estimates of willingness to pay (for an overview and extension to include the relationship between scope in valuation and scope with respect to cognition and affectation, see Heberlein et al. 2005). The scope test must be anticipated in the survey design by eliciting willingness to pay from either the same sample of respondents or two subsamples for two different quantities or qualities of the good being valued. Although asking the same sample of respondents to value two different levels of the good (an internal test) seems desirable from the neoclassical perspective because it directly controls for unmeasured individual characteristics and allows larger sample sizes, it suffers from a potential behavioral bias: the response to the first level of good tends to anchor the response to the second level, and increases the cognitive burden on the respondent. From the behavioral perspective, implementing the scope test through variation in good levels across subsamples is preferable.

When the good being valued is a reduction in mortality or morbidity risk, the appropriate scope test involves investigating whether willingness to pay is larger for larger reductions in risk. Hammitt and Graham (1999) propose a scope test for risk reductions and demonstrate its application. They argue for a strong version of the test: an approximate linear relationship between willingness to pay and probability changes. This stronger version of the test may be too strong because option price is not necessarily linear in probabilities; deviations from linearity depend on the functional from of utility. Nonetheless, recognizing probability changes as the appropriate subjects for scope tests suggests the following:

PGL 4.3 *Contingent valuation method surveys in which changes in risks are important features of the goods being valued should include, and results pass, scope tests for a positive relationship between the probabilities of desirable outcomes and willingness to pay.*

CVM surveys can potentially gather useful information for estimation and validation from questions related to uncertainty. In the referendum format it is now standard practice to ask respondents who accept bid prices how certain they are about their acceptances so that lower bounds on willingness to pay can be estimated by treating the least certain acceptances as rejections in analyses (Li and Mattsson 1995; Champ et al. 1997). Respondents may also be asked about how likely they think it is that the described public good would actually be provided as a result of their acceptance (Berrens et al. 2004). It is now common to ask questions about subjective probabilities in CVM surveys valuing goods that change risks. Respondents may be asked questions about their quantitative estimates of subjective probabilities (Andersson 2007) or, more simply, whether or not they believe their chances of experiencing an event are smaller, the same, or larger than the evidence-based probability provided to respondents (Corso 2001). As with other stated preference methods, CVM surveys should anticipate respondent heterogeneity with respect to risk. Although it would be best to take account of heterogeneity in the design process, data should be collected to allow for analysts to assess and accommodate it during analysis:

PGL 4.5 *Contingent valuation method surveys in which changes in risks are important features of the goods being valued should include questions that allow for the assessment and accommodation of heterogeneity in risk perception and preferences.*

CONCLUSION

The expected utility hypothesis assumes that individuals correctly perceive probabilities—a questionable assumption in light of considerable experimental, and some observational, evidence. As the expected utility hypothesis also plays a normative role in the assessment of efficiency, risk misperception poses challenges to CBA. One challenge, the valuation of prospects when perceived risks differ from evidence-based probabilities, seems reasonably resolved by simply using the evidence-based probabilities to calculate expected surpluses. Other challenges involve benefit transfer from revealed and stated preference studies. Recognizing these challenges, it is important for purposes of CBA to assess the benefit validity as well as the internal and external validities of existing studies. In planning studies to inform valuation, it is important to anticipate risk misperception. In the case of stated preference studies, there is an opportunity (and necessity) to improve the perception of probabilities through effective risk communication.

5

Large Deviations between WTP and WTA

Good policy analysis considers tradeoffs between the gains and losses that policies impose on people. The most common sort of tradeoff involves an increase in the quantity or quality of some good valued by people, such as access to recreation on an improved waterway, and the expenditure of the real resources needed to produce it. In such cases, CBA should value the increase in the quantity or quality of the good in terms of people's willingness to pay to obtain it. However, the tradeoff can also involve reductions in the quantity or quality of valued goods, such as loss of wilderness due to the waterway improvement. In these cases, CBA should value the decrease in the quantity or quality of the good in terms of people's willingness to accept it. In practice, however, concern about the empirical validity of WTA estimates from stated preference studies has generally led analysts to value losses in terms of people's WTP to avoid the losses instead. Indeed, this was a specific recommendation of the blue ribbon panel commissioned by the National Oceanic and Atmospheric Administration to determine the validity of contingent valuation methods for monetizing non-use losses, such as reductions in existence value, in natural resource damage assessment (Arrow et al. 1993, 4608).

Especially in predicting benefits based on stated preference methods, researchers routinely find large differences between WTA and WTP, with the former often four, five, or more times the latter. From the perspective of behavioral economics, this divergence can be explained by prospect theory. From the neoclassical perspective, such large divergences are possible for goods without close substitutes. Accepting rather than rejecting empirical estimates of WTA as having benefit validity, whether within the behavioral or neoclassic perspectives, potentially has important implications for comparing the relative efficiency of public policies (Knetsch 1990, 2015; Hammitt 2015). The objective of this chapter is to reassess the common practice of favoring WTP for measuring benefits when WTA is the conceptually correct measure.

WTA AND WTP DIVERGENCE

A study to value deer hunting permits in Wisconsin dramatically illustrates the potential divergence between WTA and WTP in both revealed and stated preference studies (Bishop and Heberlein 1990). Researchers surveyed four samples of hunters who entered a 1983 lottery to obtain permits for bagging a deer in a one-day hunt on the Sandhill research station in Wisconsin. First, in a revealed preference experiment, the WTP simulated-market sample consisted of hunters who did not initially receive permits in the lottery but were offered the opportunity to purchase them at randomly drawn prices. Second, in a stated preference experiment, the WTP contingent-value sample consisted of hunters who did not initially receive permits in the lottery but were asked if they would be willing to pay randomly drawn prices for permits if the permits were to be made available. Third, in a revealed preference experiment, the WTA simulated-market sample consisted of hunters who won permits in the lottery but were given the opportunity to sell them back at randomly drawn prices. Fourth, in a stated preference experiment, the WTA contingent-value sample consisted of hunters who won permits in the lottery but were asked if they would be willing to accept randomly drawn compensation amounts for surrendering their permits if such compensation were to be made available.

The random assignment of prices and compensation amounts allowed the researchers to estimate mean WTP and mean WTA for the market-simulation and contingent-valuation samples. Note the following results, as summarized in Table 5.1: First, with respect to WTP, the simulated-

TABLE 5.1 *Comparison of Hypothetical and Simulated Markets for Deer Hunting Permits: Willingness to Pay and Willingness to Accept (1984 dollars)*

	WTP	WTA
Simulated Market	31	153
Contingent Valuation	35	420

Source: Based on data from Bishop and Heberlein (1990, 97).

market and contingent valuation samples yielded comparable estimates of $31 and $35, respectively. Second, in the simulated-market samples, the WTA estimate of $153 is almost five times larger than the WTP estimate of $31. Third, in the contingent valuation samples, the WTA estimate of $420 was a dozen times larger than the WTP estimate of $35. If we were to take the simulated-market results as fully valid, then WTA is much larger than WTP. Further, contingent valuation provides a very good estimate of WTP but a greatly exaggerated estimate of WTA.

Such wide disparities have been observed in both experiments involving real transactions and in stated preference studies. For example, Kahneman et al. (1990) report on a series of experiments in which college students were endowed with tokens (redeemable for different amounts of money across subjects to create opportunities for gains from trade) and specific consumption goods (coffee mugs or chocolate bars). Consistent with WTAs in excess of WTPs, subjects who received the specific goods tended not to trade them as frequently as predicted. The observation of trading of tokens at predicted frequencies suggests that the failure to observe trades of the specific goods was not due to high transaction costs among subjects within the experimental setting. However, it may be possible to eliminate the gap through experimental procedures, such as providing training in using the institutional exchange mechanism before subjects provide WTP and WTA responses (Plott and Zeiler 2005).

Studies to elicit utilities for living with various chronic diseases routinely find that those with the disease report a higher quality of life than do those who are asked to anticipate having the disease (Ubel et al. 2003). As noted in Chapter 3, researchers often attribute such differences to the inability of healthy patients to anticipate their own adaptation to the disease so that their decision utility differs from their experienced utility. However, the difference is also consistent with divergence between WTA and WTP if people endowed with health (absence of the disease) are being asked questions about WTA, while people endowed with the disease are being asked about their WTP to have the disease eliminated.

A sufficiently large number of studies explicitly comparing WTA and WTP have accumulated to warrant several meta-analyses to assess the magnitude of divergence and relate it to the nature of the good being valued and the research methods employed. Horowitz and McConnell (2002) reviewed 45 studies that provided 208 experiments or surveys that produced estimates that allowed construction of the ratio of mean WTA to WTP. The mean ratio across the experiments was over 7.2; the median was 2.6. The ratio was higher for public goods and lower for ordinary private goods. Using a somewhat different set of 39 studies with 164 experiments or surveys that allowed calculation of ratios of mean WTA to mean WTP, Sayman and Öncüler (2005) report similar overall results: a mean ratio of 7.1 and a median of 2.9.

More recently, Tunçel and Hammitt (2014) reviewed 76 studies that provided 338 estimates of the ratio of mean WTA to mean WTP. Rather than report an arithmetic mean of these ratios, they report a geometric mean of 3.28, a more appropriate measure of central tendency for ratios than the arithmetic mean. For purposes of comparison with the earlier reviews, the arithmetic mean, weighted by the sample sizes of the studies, was 5.0 (e-mail communication with authors, January 29, 2015). They found a statistically significant decline in the ratio over time that was not explained solely by changes in the research design features considered. Nonetheless, researchers continue to find large disparities between WTP and WTA in many contexts.

NEOCLASSICAL EXPLANATION

Consumer surplus in a market for a private good is measured as the area between the market demand schedule, which is also the marginal valuation schedule, and price over the quantity demanded. For a linear demand schedule, the consumer surplus is the area of the familiar triangle shown in microeconomic textbooks. The benefit of a policy-induced price change is conventionally measured as the difference between the consumer surplus at the new and old prices. Again, for linear demand schedules, the change in consumer surplus is the area of the equally familiar trapezoid. Because Marshallian, or constant income, demand schedules often can be estimated empirically by relating quantity changes to changes in prices and income across time, subpopulations, or geographic locations, they can be used in practice as the basis for monetizing benefits as changes in consumer surplus.

Yet, as discussed in Chapter 2, the conceptually correct neoclassical measures of benefit are compensating variation and equivalent variation. They correspond to changes in consumer surplus, but measured using constant utility, or Hicksian, demand schedules: compensating variation is measured as a consumer surplus change based on a demand schedule that adjusts income to keep utility constant at its level prior to the price change; equivalent variation is measured as a consumer surplus change based on a demand schedule that adjusts income to keep utility constant at its level after the price change. Using feasibly estimated Marshallian demand schedules rather than the empirically elusive Hicksian demand schedules to measure changes in consumer surplus raises an obvious concern for analysts: How close do Marshallian consumer surplus changes approximate compensating and equivalent variations? The initial answers to this question led to a once widely held belief by economists that, within the neoclassical paradigm, WTP and WTA should be approximately equal.

Robert Willig (1976) addressed concerns about using Marshallian consumer surplus as a benefit measure for policy-induced price changes in market goods by deriving bounds on its deviations from compensating variation and equivalent variation. The widths of the bounds depend on the size of the consumer surplus change resulting from the price change and the income elasticity of demand, the percentage change in the quantity demanded resulting from a change in income divided by the percentage change in income, near the new and old prices. In the case of a single price change resulting in Marshallian surplus that is a small fraction of initial income, the bounds are quite tight. For example, if the ratio of the absolute value of the change in Marshallian surplus to initial income is 5 percent, then the deviation of the Marshallian surplus change from either compensating or equivalent variation is approximately 1.3 percent for an income elasticity of 0.5 and 3.8 percent for an income elasticity of 2.0 (Willig 1976, 595).

Bounding the deviations of Marshallian surplus from compensating and equivalent variation in turn bounds their deviation from each other. The Marshallian demand schedule lies between the Hicksian demand schedules, so that the magnitude of change in Marshallian surplus is between the magnitudes of changes in surplus measured using the Hicksian demand schedules. As the latter correspond to the compensating variation and equivalent variation for the price change, the magnitude of change in Marshallian surplus must be between them. Therefore, the difference between compensating variation and equivalent variation can be no larger than the sum of their maximum deviations from the change in Marshallian surplus.

Differences between compensating variation and equivalent variation correspond exactly to differences between WTP and WTA. For example, consider a policy that induces a price decrease in a market, say by reducing the cost of one of the inputs in its production. The compensating variation, the maximum amount the person could pay after the price change to return to the initial level of utility, is the WTP for this price change. The equivalent variation, the minimum amount of compensation the person would require to attain the new utility level without the policy change, is the WTA of the price change. Thus, small differences between compensating and equivalent variation imply small differences between WTP and WTA.

Although some policies, especially excise taxes and subsidies, have effects on prices in markets for traded goods, many others impose changes in the quantities of goods people consume. For example, policies may impose ceilings, including zero consumption in the case of prohibitions, or floors, such as mandated insurance, on the consumption of divisible goods traded in markets. Policies may also change consumption of the quantities of non-market goods, such as reductions in mortality risk, increasing or decreasing risk from some initial level (Viscusi 2015b). Particularly in environmental policy applications, the goods may be nonrivalrous, like preservation of a species, such that every person must consume the same quantity. How closely do changes in Marshallian consumer surplus approximate compensating variation and equivalent variation, and therefore WTP and WTA, when policies induce quantity changes?

To answer this question, Alan Randall and John Stoll (1980) constructed a framework in which policy affects the quantities of goods consumed directly rather than indirectly through price changes. Within this framework, rather than the divergence between WTP and WTA depending on the income elasticity of demand, it depends on the price flexibility of income, which is defined as the percentage change in marginal valuation resulting from a change in income divided by the percentage change in income when no changes in the quantity of the good can be made. The bounds they derived have the same form as those derived by Willig (1976) for price changes, but with income elasticity of demand replaced by the price flexibility of income and the change in consumer surplus measured over the change in quantity rather than the change in price.

Specifically, they derive an approximation of the following form:

$$(\text{WTA} - \text{WTP})/A \cong \xi A/Y \qquad \text{(EQ. 5.1)}$$

where ξ is the price flexibility, A is the Marshallian surplus change, and Y is the total budget available before the policy change. The left-hand side of Equation 5.1, the difference between WTA and WTP as a percentage of the surplus change, will be small for small changes in surplus and small values of price flexibility.

   Randall and Stoll (1980) were very careful in pointing out that either large surplus changes relative to income or large values of price flexibility could result in large deviations of WTP and WTA from Marshallian surplus changes and therefore from each other. Nonetheless, economists tended to view their article primarily as an extension of the Willig results to policy-induced quantity changes, and therefore consistent with an expectation that differences between WTP and WTA should generally be small. If one were to assume that price flexibility has a comparable magnitude to the more familiar income elasticity of demand (the percentage change in the quantity demanded resulting from a one percentage point increase in income), then this view is reasonable. Thus, the defense of Marshallian surplus changes as approximations of the correct neoclassical benefit metrics set the stage for the large differences between WTP and WTA found in empirical work to be viewed as a fundamental challenge to the neoclassical paradigm.

   The bounds developed by Randall and Stoll, like those of Willig, depend only on the income effect, operating either through induced changes in real income in the case of price changes and price flexibility in the case of quantity changes. W. Michael Hanemann (1991) extended the analysis to take account of the ease with which market goods could be substituted for the good being valued. Specifically, he considered the substitution effect in this context to "mean the ease with which other privately marketed commodities can be substituted for the given public good or fixed commodity, while maintaining the individual at a constant level of utility"(p. 635). The absence of close substitutes creates a large gap between WTP and WTA because the former is bounded by income but the latter may require very large increases in expenditures on the poor substitutes to restore the original level of utility.

   Hanemann's primary result showed the dependency of price flexibility in the Randall and Stoll bounds on the availability of market substitutes. Specifically, he showed that

$$\xi = {}^{\eta}/_{\sigma_o} \qquad\qquad \text{(EQ. 5.2)}$$

where ξ is the price flexibility, η is the income elasticity of demand, and σ_o is the Allen-Uzawa elasticity of substitution between the good being valued and a composite of other goods. The price flexibility is non-negatively unbounded because the elasticity of substitution is non-negatively unbounded. For example, the elasticity of substitution might be extremely large for a policy that restricted the sale of super-sized beverages because it would be relatively easy to substitute multiple purchases of the still available but smaller-sized beverages. In this case, the price flexibility would be extremely small, so that by Equation 5.1, the difference between WTP and WTA would also be very small. However, with respect to a policy that changed the availability of a rare scenic area, such as flooding the Yosemite Valley to make a lake like the nearby Hetch Hetchy Reservoir, many individuals may have utility functions with close to zero substitutability with market goods so that the price flexibility would approach infinity and therefore so would their differences between WTP and WTA.

BEHAVIORAL EXPLANATION

Both before and after Hanemann's demonstration of the possibility of very large divergences between WTP and WTA within the neoclassical paradigm, behavioral economists offered, and continue to offer, an alternative explanation based on prospect theory: respondents are valuing gains and losses from their reference points differently. Specifically, as illustrated in Figure 4.1, a gain increases an individual's valuation score less than a loss of the same magnitude decreases it (violating BERA3). The reference point, which should be irrelevant from the neoclassical perspective, plays a central role in the behavioral explanation. In revealing preferences, individuals bring to the decision beliefs that affect their reference points; in stating preferences, individuals may formulate beliefs that affect their reference points based on the way elicitations are framed.

Building on a classification set out by Zerbe (2001), Knetsch et al. (2012) identify four different metrics for welfare changes. As displayed in Table 5.2, the metrics depend on whether the policy produces either a positive or a negative change and whether the individual's reference

TABLE 5.2 *Valuing Positive and Negative Changes*

	Positive Change	Negative Change
Compensating Variation (reference: before change)	WTP for gaining better outcome	WTA worse outcome
Equivalent Variation (reference: after change)	WTA forgoing better outcome	WTP to avoid worse outcome

Source: Adapted from Knetsch et al. (2012), table 1, page 9.

point is the situation either before or after the policy change. Consider, for example, the valuation of a policy that would make the positive change of cleaning up an oil spill. If the individual takes the current situation, oil in the water, as the reference point, then cleaning it up would be appropriately measured as a WTP based on compensating variation (upper left cell of Table 5.2). However, if the individual saw clean water as the reference point, then the cleanup would be valued as the WTA forgoing the cleanup based on equivalent variation (lower left cell). Now assume that a spill has not yet occurred but that this negative change will occur in the absence of a preventive policy. If the individual takes clean water as the reference point, then the valuation of the preventive measure would be valued in terms of a WTA an oil spill based on compensating variation (upper right cell). However, if the individual takes oil in the water as the reference point, then the valuation of the preventive measure would be in terms of WTP based on equivalent variation (lower right cell).

What determines individuals' reference points? Individuals may take current reality as the reference point. That is, they may assess gains and losses relative to the allocation that currently exists and would remain in the absence of an intervening policy. For example, if oil drilling fouls their wells, then the reference point is the unusable water. Consistent with a legal perspective on damages, their reference point may be based instead on formal property rights. Thus, if they have a property right to clean well water, they would assess gains and losses relative to the reference point of clean water even after the water has been fouled. However, psychologically, they may perceive a property right that they do not legally hold—although they do not have a legal right to clean well water, they perceive that morally they have this right and again assess gains and losses after the fouling of the wells relative to clean water. Whereas the current reality and legal perspectives determine specific reference points, the psychological perspective depends on the beliefs and values of the particular individual.

Two very different normative interpretations of reference points have been offered. First, from a legal perspective, some argue that the determination of reference points should be based solely on the allocation of property rights rather than perceived property rights (Levy and Friedman 1994). This view seems most appropriate from the perspective of determining compensation for damages that have occurred, both in terms of fairness as well as making property rights effective in promoting the efficient use of resources by the rights holders. However, the ex-post assessment of legal damages is not the same as ex-ante prediction of the benefits of policy changes. Therefore, I argue that the property rights perspective does not provide the correct framing for CBA.

Second, Zerbe (2001) argues that, properly interpreting the meaning of WTP and WTA, psychological rather than purely legal reference points are appropriate. This argument has merit in the sense that we could legitimately assess benefits by using either compensating or equivalent variation. Indeed, as discussed in Chapter 2, strict application of the Kaldor–Hicks–Scitovsky criterion would require the analyst to assess benefits in terms of both of these measures to determine whether a policy change would be unequivocally efficient. The practical problem, however, is that we generally measure benefits using only compensating variation. Although we could choose to measure benefits by either the upper row (compensating variation) or the lower row (equivalent variation) in Table 5.2, consistency with our other measures of costs and benefits argues for staying in the top row. Basing benefit assessment on compensating variation requires that elicitations should be framed so that current reality is the reference point.

Accepting current reality as the appropriate reference point in stated preference studies leads to the following practical guideline:

PGL 5.1 *Consistently apply compensating variation using WTP for policies that provide gains to the individual and WTA for policies that impose losses on the individual.*

This guideline rejects the psychological perspective on reference points advocated by many behavioral economists because of its indeterminacy and possible mixing of benefit measures. It also rejects the common admonition to frame all elicitations in terms of WTP (using either the upper left or lower right cells in Table 5.2) because of its mixing of benefit measures.

WTA BENEFIT VALIDITY

A fundamental concern remains about the validity of WTA estimates that are grossly larger than their WTP counterparts. Consider first the neoclassical perspective. As discussed, a key determinant of the divergence between WTP and WTA is price flexibility, which in turn depends on not only income elasticity but also the substitutability of market goods for the good being valued. Public goods, such as unique environmental amenities, may have very low substitutability so that the difference between WTP and WTA could be immense. Indeed, if no substitution were possible, then the difference could approach infinity. For example, a policy that eliminated an especially majestic scenic view might require an extremely large amount of compensation to return an individual to her level of utility before the view was eliminated.

The possibility of an unbounded WTA poses a fundamental conceptual challenge to CBA. On the one hand, CBA should reflect the valuations of all individuals with standing so that all WTA values should be acceptable. On the other hand, accepting an infinite, or even just extremely large, WTA for any one individual would effectively give that person a veto over any policy determined on the basis of efficiency. An extremely large WTA would turn consumer sovereignty into consumer dictatorship by swamping WTP amounts for positive impacts of the policy, which are bounded by individuals' incomes. Recognizing that CBA is a protocol for assessing efficiency rather than a decision rule provides some flexibility in the way that extreme WTP amounts might be reasonably handled.

One approach is to estimate net benefits for different bounds on WTA to convey efficiency but also estimate the fraction of the population with WTA estimates above the bound to register extreme valuations. For example, imagine that analysts estimate WTA amounts for a representative sample of the population with standing and that the tail of the distribution includes estimates sufficiently large to make other costs and benefit estimates irrelevant for determining the sign of net benefits. The analysts could calculate net benefits by limiting the magnitude of WTA at various levels and successively censoring larger WTAs to be no greater than these levels. At each censoring level, the fraction of respondents whose WTA was censored would be reported along with the net benefit. A related approach would be to answer the question with a break-even analysis: When net benefit using unbounded WTA amounts is negative, is there any bound greater that WTP that would result in zero net benefit? If such a bound exists, then it would be reported along with the fraction of the population with WTA amounts above this bound; its magnitude and the fraction of the population with larger WTA amounts would provide information on the likely efficiency of the policy. If no such bound exists, then the CBA could be interpreted as indicating that, subject to uncertainties in the prediction of other parameters, the policy would not be efficient.

As very large difference between WTP and WTA are also possible within the behavioral framework, the above discussion suggests the following guideline:

PGL 5.2 *To preserve the value of CBA in assessing efficiency when extremely large values of WTA dominate net benefits, the sensitivity of net benefits to WTA bounds should be calculated and presented along with estimates of the fractions of the population with values above the bounds.*

The behavioral perspective, however, raises an additional question for neoclassical CBA: Are benefits meaningful if individuals value policy changes according to prospect theory rather than neoclassical utility theory? Clearly, individuals whose behaviors are consistent with prospect theory are stating WTP and WTA amounts for the policy changes being considered. The question is not so much whether these values themselves can be treated as valid, but rather whether their very acceptance challenges the validity of the neoclassical framework to such a degree as to bring into question any neoclassical benefit measures. As much evidence for doing CBA comes from preferences revealed in various institutional settings, one can make arguments like those in Chapter 4 about the mitigating effects of markets on behaviors that violate neoclassical axioms. Lacking a better answer myself, but nonetheless remaining convinced of the practical value of CBA, including the analytical discipline it requires, I leave it to others to provide their own answers.

At least in one important application, revealed preference evidence shows only a small divergence between WTP and WTA. Kniesner et al. (2014) focus on workers who change jobs. Some workers accepted jobs with higher mortality risks and higher wages (WTA); other workers accepted jobs with lower mortality risks and lower wages (WTP). Although the WTA estimates were generally larger than the WTP estimates, they were larger by less than about 20 percent and were not statistically significantly different across a number of model specifications. This finding suggests that the laboratory divergence between WTP and WTA may not be large for experienced participants in well-developed markets. Unfortunately, revealed preference estimates are often unavailable for CBA.

IMPLICATIONS FOR STATED PREFERENCE METHODS

Another question has more immediate relevance to practice: How do we decide on the appropriate framing of elicitations of WTP and WTA in stated reference studies? As discussed in Chapter 3, the behavioral welfare economics of Bernheim and Rangel (2009) allows for the influence of ancillary conditions that affect people's choices but are not considered to be welfare relevant. Ancillary conditions may result in individuals' psychological reference points deviating from current reality. For example, in valuing the cleanup of a hypothetical oil spill, a person's reference point may be unspoiled water to which he or she feels entitled, say because of the way culpability for an actual spill was recently presented in the news media, rather than the hypothetically fouled water. Therefore, among the other informational burdens facing stated preference researchers is providing information to move the psychological reference point closer to the hypothetical status quo.

The inherent hypothetical nature of WTP and WTA elicitation in stated preference methods opens the door for ancillary conditions to influence responses to elicitation questions. Much stated preference craft, informed by behavioral findings and criticism almost since its inception, has evolved to improve respondents' understanding of the hypothetical choice and to increase the chances that they will treat the choice as an economic decision involving a relevant tradeoff (Loomis 2014). For example, in addition to the mandatory budget reminder embedded within WTP elicitations, respondents may be primed to think about tradeoffs through earlier questions about discretionary income (Li et al. 2005). More recent research emphasizes the importance of respondents believing that there is some chance that their elicitation response could influence policy (Vossler et al. 2012), the assessment of respondent certainty through follow-up questions (Blumenschein et al. 2008), and the request for oaths from respondents (Jacquemet et al. 2013).

Although the discussion has so far concerned the conceptual validity of large differences between WTP and WTA, hypothetical biases and other challenges to valid elicitation raise measurement issues. Large differences are conceptually plausible, especially if the good does not have close substitutes. Returning to Table 5.1, the 5:1 ratio of WTA to WTP in the first row, which presents revealed preference results from simulated markets, is plausible because of the limited opportunity to hunt in previously restricted areas and the absence of other deer hunting opportunities on that particular day. Taking the revealed preference estimates of WTA and WTP as valid, however, raises concerns about stated preference estimates, which overestimate WTA by a factor of almost three. Because many important policy impacts cannot be feasibly assessed with revealed preference methods, the apparent gross overestimation of the magnitude of WTA in stated preference studies brings into question the feasibility of its use.

The most recent review of studies that estimated both WTA and WTP included regressions to assess the impacts of various study characteristics on their ratio (Tunçel and Hammitt 2014). Two study features appear to reduce the ratio of WTA to WTP. First, relevant both to studies involving real transactions (revealed preferences) and hypothetical transactions (stated preferences), experience either with the market for the good, when it exists, or with the experimental situation reduced the ratio. The former is not relevant in stated preference studies when the purpose is to value non-market goods. The latter is more relevant because it can be made part of the elicitation protocol. For example, as discussed in Chapter 4, showing respondents the consequences of irrational valuations of lotteries for private goods may have spillover effects to public good valuations (Cherry et al. 2003).

Second, stated preference studies that employed "incentive-compatible" elicitation formats had smaller ratios—incentive compatible is in quotes because the available formats generally reduce but do not necessarily eliminate strategic responses. Building on results from the theory of mechanism design, Carson and Groves (2007) argue that any elicitation format that allows individuals to express more than a binary choice facilitates strategic responses. Only the simple dichotomous choice elicitation format immediately meets this criterion. Further, if respondents believe that they would actually have to pay the bid prices for bids they accept, then the dichotomous choice elicitation mechanism is incentive compatible and therefore will elicit truthful responses in WTP elicitations. (The dichotomous choice elicitation, however, is not necessarily incentive compatible for WTA elicitations even when respondents believe they would receive accepted compensations.) Open-ended (respondents state amounts) or payment card (respondents pick amounts from lists) elicitation formats do not present respondents with a binary choice and therefore permit strategic behavior. However, these methods can be made *more* incentive compatible if they are combined with some mechanism to encourage respondents to state their preferences more truthfully (Vickery 1961; Becker et al. 1964; Goves and Ledyard 1977; Smith 1980). For example, Brookshire and Coursey (1987) combine an open-ended elicitation format for the valuation of tree densities in a park with statements relating the WTP and WTA amounts expressed by individuals to the realization of the density changes. In the WTP scenario, the increased tree density would not be provided unless the WTP amounts of all respondents surpassed a threshold; in the WTA scenario, neither the decreased tree density nor the compensation payments would be provided unless the WTA amounts of all respondents fell below a threshold. The use of this mechanism did not reduce the ratio of WTA to WTP in the single-shot field experiments but did reduce it in a laboratory setting with repetition.

Stated preference methods ask respondents to make economic decisions. In the case of WTP elicitations, it is important that respondents view the bid prices they accept as reducing the amount of money they would have available to spend on other things (Arrow et al. 1993). The so-called budget reminder plays an essential role in helping respondents adopt an economic framing of their decision. It typically appears in the elicitation question itself. For example, if the respondent has been offered a bid price of $t for an environmental regulation that would increase energy prices, then the elicitation question would include a statement like the following: "Keep in mind that [t] dollars spent on increased energy and gasoline prices could not be spent on other things, such as other household expenses, charities, groceries, or car payments" (Berrens et al. 2004, 337). In general practice, the payment vehicle, the mechanism through which individuals are asked to anticipate payment, matches the way the good would be financed, typically either as higher prices of goods, as in the example, or as additional tax payments.

It may be possible to prime economic responses to the WTP question with refined budget reminders prior to elicitations. To reduce cognitive demands, consumers appear to employ a two-stage process in making purchasing decisions, first setting up a number of mental accounts for categories of purchases and then making decisions within these accounts (Deaton and Muellbauer 1980). For example, Bateman and Langford (1997) primed a mental account for recreation by asking respondents about their recreational expenditures. Li et al. (2005) employed a similar approach, first asking respondents about their monthly discretionary expenditures and then about their donations to environmental causes—the median household WTP for the sample of respondents who were primed in this way was 50–60 percent lower than for the sample of respondents just receiving the standard budget reminder in the elicitation question.

Respondents' recognition of their own budget constraints thus plays an important role in the elicitation of WTP by helping them address hypothetical choices as if they were economic decisions. In WTA elicitation, however, respondents do not face individual budget constraints (Vortherms 2014). Greater compensation does not involve making tradeoffs against their consumption of other goods. Indeed, greater compensation would allow consumption of more of other goods.

Absent meaningful private budget constraints, some researchers have used so-called social budget constraints in WTA elicitations to encourage economic choices by respondents (Mäntymaa 1999). Situations in which the hypothetical compensation would come from a government provide the most straightforward application: prior to the elicitation, respondents are reminded that the compensation they receive will not be available for other public uses. For example, del Saz-Salazar et al. (2012) ask respondents about their willingness to accept reductions in property taxes as compensation for the negative externalities that would accompany expansion of a Spanish port. Respondents were reminded that reductions in property taxes would result in less spending on public services. This social budget reminder encourages thinking in terms of tradeoffs. However, the tradeoff between compensation and government spending is much more removed from common experience than a tradeoff between WTP and routine consumption. The tradeoff with government spending requires respondents to assess their own valuations of the loss to society from the forgone expenditures.

In dichotomous choice elicitation, a complication arises if the social budget constraint is effective. Rejection of a bid could mean that it did not provide enough compensation. It could also mean that the respondent thought the bid offered too much compensation in terms of expense to the commonweal. Follow-up questions would be required to determine the rationale for bid rejection so high-bid rejection could be appropriately taken into account in estimating mean or median WTA for the sample.

As none of the simple WTA elicitation formats are incentive compatible, including the dichotomous choice method, the sort of information conveyed by the social budget constraint might be incorporated into the auxiliary mechanism used to encourage truthful revelation. The Brookshire and Coursey (1987) study of WTA for lower tree densities illustrates this approach. A more recent example is provided by Krishna et al. (2013) in their assessment of farmers' WTA amounts for substituting more ecologically beneficial varieties of millet for the varieties with the highest private return that are currently being planted. Prior to the elicitation question, respondents were informed that "before you answer, please note that *only* a limited number of households in the Kolli Hills would be selected to participate in this scheme, as the amount of funding for the scheme would be limited. Therefore, the smaller the amount of support you would require to participate in the programme, the higher are your chances of being selected" (p. 114).

How effective are these sorts of mechanisms in enabling stated preference studies to produce meaningful estimates of WTA? Unfortunately, a confident answer is not possible. The finding of Tunçel and Hammitt (2014) that incentive-compatible elicitation formats reduced the ratio of WTA to WTP was based on only 7 out of 167 observations of ratios from stated preference studies. Surveys that elicit WTA, like those of the nearby port residents and millet farmers, generally have not employed split-sample experiments to assess the impact of the versions of the social budget constraint/incentive compatibility mechanism they employ—contingent valuation studies are expensive, so splitting samples is often not financially feasible with limited research budgets. More research is need. However, while we wait for the results of that research, using WTA when conceptually appropriate, as called for in PGL 5.1, almost always requires the use of stated preference methods:

PGL 5.3 *Stated preference methods to elicit WTA should employ "incentive-compatible" social budget constraint framings with follow-up questions to assess respondents' perceptions of tradeoffs.*

If the elicitation is to provide meaningful estimates of WTA, then respondents must be making economic decisions in the sense of confronting tradeoffs. This suggests two sorts of follow-up questions: First, would they consider any level of compensation for the loss? If the answer is no, then we return to the situation previously discussed, in which accepting this answer at face value renders CBA uninformative. Negative answers provide information that may be useful in applying the methods suggested in PGL 5.2; positive answers reinforce confidence that respondents are making economic decisions. Second, how do respondents view the social budget constraint? Its effectiveness in encouraging economic decisions depends on the marginal value they place on public expenditures. Positive marginal values encourage economic framing, while zero or negative marginal values do not.

The discussion so far has been from the perspective of the "ingredients" approach to CBA, in which the change in the quality or quantity of a particular good, such as an environmental amenity, is being valued. The focus on a single impact facilitates the reasonable assumption that everyone shares either a non-negative valuation of the change (making WTP appropriate) or a non-positive valuation of the change (making WTA appropriate). For example, although some people might not be willing to pay anything for improved water quality in a particular lake, it is reasonable to assume that no one would demand compensation to accept the improved quality willingly; similarly, although someone might not demand compensation for a decrease in air quality in a national park, it is reasonable to assume that no one would be willing to pay to obtain the decrease.

The assumption that all people view a proposed change as either not a loss or not a gain typically becomes implausible when we change perspective from ingredients to policy "meals," because alternative policies typically have multiple impacts that could on net be valued positively by some people and negatively by others. Contingent valuation employing the standard referendum format when preferences are heterogeneous in this way would result either in those with negative valuations of the policy change rejecting all bids in WTP elicitations or those with positive valuations of the policy change accepting any level of compensation in WTA elicitations. Therefore, although valuations of alternative policies with multiple impacts would provide information directly relevant to policy decisions, preference heterogeneity would bring into question the use of either WTP or WTA.

Carlson et al. (2016) propose a modification of contingent valuation for assessing the efficiency of current policy relative to a single alternative. The first step employs a question to segregate respondents into those who favor current policy and those who favor the alternative independent of financial considerations for their households. The alternative not selected is assumed to establish the reference utility level for each of the two groups of respondents. The second step employs separate referendum elicitations to estimate the WTP of each group for its preferred alternative relative to the one rejected. The third step assesses the relative efficiency of alternatives to current policy as the difference in the average WTP of the former minus the average WTP of the latter.

The innovation of dividing respondents according to policy preferences to create homogenous groups seems to be necessary for valuing complete policies with multiple impacts. As one can argue that current policy should not be privileged over possible alternatives, there is a logic to defining reference points in terms of respondents' policy preferences so that WTP elicitation can be employed for each group. Of course, the logic would also allow for specifying the desired policy as the reference point so that WTA the rejected policy would be the appropriate elicitation, which could lead to a different assessment of relative efficiency. Determining when the choice of preferred policy rather than not preferred policy as the reference point could reverse the assessment of relative efficiency is desirable but empirically challenging because of the difficulties of implementing WTA elicitations.

CONCLUSION

The commonly observed large gap between WTA and WTP has been a focal point in debates between advocates of the behavioral and neoclassical paradigms. Initially viewed as a neoclassical anomaly, the gap has posed the most prominent behavioral challenge to CBA, especially with respect to the use of stated preference methods to measure benefits. Although the behavioral explanation, based on individuals valuing gains and losses from reference points rather than valuing outcomes, continues to provide a plausible explanation for the gap, its necessity became less urgent with the realization that the neoclassical perspective also allows very large values of WTA for policy outcomes involving reductions in goods that individuals view as having poor substitutes. Nonetheless, behavioral economics has direct implications for improving stated preference methods, such as the importance of helping respondents establish appropriate reference points, increasing their familiarity with the elicitation process, and heightening their awareness of economic tradeoffs.

6

Non-Exponential Time Discounting

The first applications of CBA assessed dams, harbors, canals, roadways, and other infrastructure projects that require substantial expenditures of resources to construct but then provide benefits over long periods of time often measured in decades. Social policies that affect human capital often have impacts over people's lifetimes. Environmental policies, such as the preservation of habitats for endangered species, responses to global climate change, or the storage of nuclear waste, may have impacts over centuries. The standard practice for discounting the costs and benefits predicted to accrue in the future relative to those incurred immediately rests on two related concepts: First, people, and therefore society, prefer consumption sooner rather than later. The so-called marginal rate of pure time preference indicates how people trade consumption today for consumption sometime in the future. Second, use of resources today for public projects reduces private investment that would have enabled future consumption—the so-called marginal rate of return on private investment. In the ideal neoclassical world of perfect capital markets these two concepts lead to discounting at the same rate, the market rate of interest, but in the world in which we actually live they suggest different rates. Although the appropriate concept, and therefore the rate, for discounting has been controversial, its application through an exponential function in conventional CBA has been uncontroversial.

Exponential discounting follows immediately from the definition of the marginal rate of return on private investment. It also follows from a common assumption, almost universally employed in neoclassical economics: that the global utility an individual receives from intertemporal consumption can be expressed as the sum of exponentially discounted utilities in all time periods. A very important practical reason for embracing exponential discounting of utility is that it allows consumption and real resource costs to be discounted using the same procedure. An important theoretical reason is that only exponential discounting guarantees that intertemporal preferences are time consistent, which in this context means that the ordering of outcomes accruing at a fixed difference in time does not depend on how far in the future the orderings occur (Strotz 1955–56). Basically, because the exponential function has no "memory," the amount the utility of consumption one year in the future beyond any selected year is discounted does not depend on when the assessment is made.

Considerable behavioral evidence suggests that in many situations individuals do not make choices as if they were maximizing global utility based on exponentially discounted period-specific utilities (Loewenstein and Prelec 1992; Frederick et al. 2002). It often appears that individuals apply much larger discounts in near-term decisions than they do in making longer-run comparisons (O'Donoghue and Rabin 2015). The choices in these situations of immediate impatience, or "temptation," are better described (and often better predicted) by assuming that individuals are discounting according to a hyperbolic, quasi-hyperbolic, or other non-exponential function (in violation of BERA7). What are the implications of such non-exponential discounting of utility for CBA?

Answering this question begins with a clarification of the neoclassical discounting concepts and their underlying assumptions. It then requires two assessments of the implications of non-exponential discounting of utility. First, accepting predictions of future costs and benefits at face value, is exponential discounting of net benefits appropriate? Second, what are the implications of non-exponential discounting for benefit validity? In particular, when do public policy interventions that induce decisions more consistent with exponential discounting actually produce benefits?

DISCOUNTING WITH PERFECT CAPITAL MARKETS

A simple two-period analysis illustrates the concepts underlying discounting. Figure 6.1 shows production and consumption in the first period on the horizontal axis and production and consumption in the second period on the vertical axis. In the absence of a capital market, a situation of personal autarky, the consumer can choose to produce, and therefore consume, at any point on or inside the curve connecting points X_1 and X_2. The points on

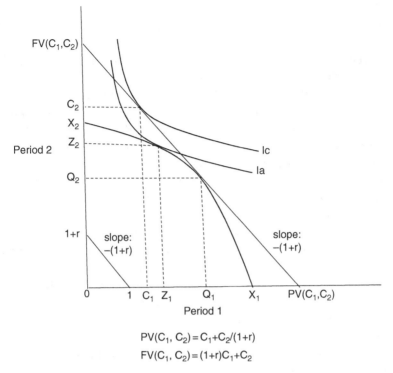

$$PV(C_1, C_2) = C_1 + C_2/(1+r)$$
$$FV(C_1, C_2) = (1+r)C_1 + C_2$$

FIGURE 6.1 Present Values and Discounting

the curve define the person's production possibility frontier. Once on the production possibility frontier, producing more in the first period (moving toward X_1) requires her to give up increasingly more in the second period. For example, working more in the first period at the expense of investing in her own human capital would reduce how much she can produce in the second period. The slope of a line tangent to the curve at any point indicates the rate at which she can trade production, and therefore consumption, in the two periods. To maximize utility, she would select the point on the production possibility frontier that would allow her to reach her highest feasible indifference curve. In the diagram, indifference curve I_a is just tangent to the production possibility frontier and would allow her to produce and consume Z_1 in the first period and Z_2 in the second period. The slope of the indifference curve at this point is both her marginal rate of return on investment in the first period and her marginal rate of pure time preference, the rate at which she is willing to trade marginal changes in consumption between the two periods.

Now imagine that this person has access to a capital market in which she could borrow or lend at an interest rate, r. Looking to the lower, left-hand section of the figure, the diagonal interest-rate line between 1 unit on the horizontal axis and 1+r on the vertical axis represents all the combinations of consumption she could have in the two periods if she began with 1 in the first period, 1+r in the second period, or any point on the line in between. Any of these starting points would allow her to move anywhere on the line through borrowing or lending. For example, if she had 1 unit in the first period, she could lend it and receive 1+r in the second period. The existence of the capital market means that a line with the same slope, −(1+r) along which she can choose consumption combinations, runs through any point she can achieve through her own production.

With the availability of the capital market, she can now maximize utility by increasing first-period production from Z_1 to Q_1, lending Q_1-C_1, and then consuming $Q_2+(1+r)(Q_1-C_1)$ in the second period. In the figure, producing at (Q_1,Q_2) allows her to move along the interest-rate line to consume (at C_1 and C_2) on indifference curve I_c. If she had wanted all her consumption to be in the second period, then she could have moved all the way to the point on the vertical axis labeled $FV(C_1,C_2)$, the future value of this combination of consumption (and also the future value of the production quantities, Q_1 and Q_2.) Alternatively, if she had wanted all her consumption in the first period, she could have moved all the way to the point on the horizontal axis labeled $PV(C_1,C_2)$, the present value of this combination of consumption (and also the present value of the production quantities, Q_1 and Q_2.)

Note that the point on the production possibility frontier that maximizes the present value of consumption (or production) also maximizes utility by allowing the person to reach the highest possible indifference curve. This is the intuition behind using the present value of net benefits to compare policy alternatives. Algebraically, the present value consists of two components. First, it includes actual consumption in the first period, C_1. Second, it includes the addition to first-period consumption that could be obtained by borrowing against all future consumption to obtain an additional $C_2/(1+r)$ in first-period consumption. The resulting expression:

$$PV(C1, C2) = C_1 + C_2/(1 + r) \qquad \text{(Eq. 6.1)}$$

is the familiar two-period discounting formula. The r is referred to as the discount rate; $1/(1+r)$ is referred to as the discount factor.

The logic can be extended to multiple periods. So, if we wanted the present value for three periods, we would first find the present value starting in the second period, $C_2 + C_3/(1+r)$, where C_3 is the third period consumption. Now finding the present value starting in the first period, we have $C_1 + [C_2 + C_3/(1+r)]/(1+r)$, or $C_1 + C_2/(1+r) + C_3/(1+r)^2$. For N periods, the formula becomes

$$PV(C_1, C_2, \ldots, C_N) = \sum_{n=1}^{N} \frac{C_n}{(1+r)^{n-1}} \qquad \text{(EQ. 6.2)}$$

As the lengths of the periods approach zero, the formula approaches an exponential distribution, hence the term "exponential discounting." CBA uses the above formula for calculating the present value of net benefits. The nuts and bolts of discounting typically involve projecting net benefits in real dollars by valuing predicted impacts with current prices and applying a real discount rate; valuing continuous flows of costs and benefits mid-period; annualizing net benefits to compare projects of different lengths; and appropriately valuing scrap values at the terminations of projects (Boardman et al. 2011).

Generalizing the analysis in Figure 6.1 to more than two periods in this way, however, requires an additional assumption: the individual's marginal rate of pure time preference remains constant over successive periods. In the two-period analysis, any utility function that yields the indifference curves supports the analysis. In moving to multiple periods, however, the utility function must be restricted to satisfy the assumption. A particular restriction, introduced as an expediency by Paul Samuelson (1937), explicitly imposes exponential discounting on a time separable utility function. Specifically, utility in each period is assumed to depend only on consumption in that period and overall, or global, utility taking account of all future periods is the exponentially discounted sum of period-specific utilities summed over periods. The assumption of such exponentially discounted utility is ubiquitous in neoclassical analysis.

The key point from this idealized analysis is that with the existence of a perfect capital market, utility is maximized when the marginal rate of return on private investment equals r and the marginal rate of pure time preference equals r. So, whether we base the present value on the marginal rate of pure time preference or the marginal rate of return on private investment, we would discount using the market interest rate r (either assuming no general price inflation or adjusted for inflation to be a real interest rate). If everyone in the economy had access to this ideal capital market, then everyone would equate their marginal rates of pure time preference and their marginal rates of return on private investment to the same quantity, r. We would therefore refer to r as the social discount rate. It would be the appropriate rate for finding the present value of net benefits, the metric we use to compare alternatives in CBA.

Unfortunately, a perfect capital market does not exist. Further, various taxes, transaction costs, and market distortions create a gap between the marginal rate of pure time preference and the marginal rate of return on private investment. For the US economy, estimates of the long-term marginal rate of pure time preference are about 1–4 percent and estimates of the long-term marginal rate of return on private investment are about 5–8 percent (Moore et al. 2004; Burgess and Zerbe 2011; Moore et al. 2013a). The gap is consequential because the social discount rate can have a large effect on the predicted present value of net benefits of projects with long time horizons when a mismatch occurs between the timing of costs and benefits, which is typically the case for investments in physical or human capital. Not surprisingly in view of its importance for present values, the appropriate basis for, and therefore the assumed value of, the social discount rate remains controversial.

Economists advocating for use of the marginal rate of return on private investment as the social discount rate see government investments as funded from borrowing that crowds out private investment through higher interest rates. If government expenditures on projects reduce private investment dollar for dollar, then the marginal rate of return on private investment appropriately captures the opportunity cost of the expenditures and therefore is the appropriate social discount rate (Burgess and Zerbe 2011, 2013).

Economists advocating for basing the social discount rate on the marginal rate of pure time preference see government investments as funded by taxes that primarily reduce consumption. If government expenditures on projects reduce consumption dollar for dollar, then the marginal rate of pure time preference appropriately captures the opportunity cost of the expenditures and therefore is the appropriate basis for the social discount rate (Moore et al. 2013b). Following the seminal work of Frank P. Ramsey (1928) on growth theory, these advocates would adjust the marginal rate of pure time preference to take account of any social preferences for smoother consumption over time—recognizing that future generations will be wealthier and therefore have higher levels of per capita consumption, they argue for a social discount rate somewhat higher than the marginal rate of pure time preference.

A conceptually valid but largely unused method for reconciling the gap between the marginal rate of return on private investment and the marginal rate of pure time preference employs the shadow price of capital to value changes in investment in terms of the changes in the present value of consumption they induce (Bradford 1975; Lyon 1990; Boardman et al. 2011). The shadow price of capital depends on both the marginal rate of return on private investment and the marginal rate of pure time preference, as well as the savings rate and the rate of depreciation. In each period, costs and benefits are divided into those that affect consumption and those that affect investment. The shadow price of capital is then applied to the net changes in investment to convert them to their equivalent changes in consumption. This conversion expresses all impacts in terms of consumption so that discounting at the marginal rate of pure time preference is appropriate.

In practice, although reasonable assumptions about the economy-wide savings and depreciation rates can be employed to develop plausible shadow prices, analysts rarely have sufficient information to partition impacts between those that affect investment and those that affect consumption. Consequently, analysts must choose between the two warring camps. Governments typically provide guidance to their analysts on the choice. For example, the Office of Management and Budget recommends that Regulatory Impact Analyses use real discount rates of 3 and 7 percent (US OMB 2003). The recommended rates in the United Kingdom, Germany, and France are 3.5 percent, 3 percent, and 4 percent, respectively (Moore et al. 2013a). My own view favors a social discount rate based on the marginal rate of pure time preference, and therefore is consistent with the lower rate suggested by the Office of Management and Budget, because ultimately all government debt must be repaid with revenue from taxes (Moore et al. 2013b). However, consistent with this approach is the recognition that taxes generally impose inefficiencies on the economy. The marginal excess tax burden captures these inefficiencies (Ballard et al. 1985; Dahlby 2008) and therefore should be applied to changes in government revenue (Vining and Weimer 2010).

In summary, neoclassical CBA discounts costs and benefits exponentially. In terms of costs, exponential discounting follows immediately from opportunities to trade expenditures on real resources across time periods through borrowing or lending. In terms of benefits, it follows from the assumption that intertemporal utility can be written as a global utility equal to an exponentially discounted sum of period-specific utilities. At least with respect to intragenerational discounting, on-going and often heated controversy about discounting has not been about the validity of exponential discounting, but rather about the social discount rate used to implement it. Even concern that discounting at rates appropriate for time horizons within a generation result in virtually no weight being placed on costs and benefits borne by future generations has been addressed within the exponential discounting framework. If the appropriate rate for use in discounting the far future is uncertain, then only the smallest of the possible rates will dominate the calculation of present values (Weitzman 1998). Recognition of this process supports the use of a lower discount rate in intergenerational than intragenerational discounting (Moore et al. 2004; Gollier and Hammitt 2014). So too do intergenerational growth models that show optimally lower rates of return to public than private investment (Robson and Szentes 2014). Indeed, France and the United Kingdom specify schedules of declining discount rates to be applied to projects with long time horizons (Arrow et al. 2012).

NON-EXPONENTIAL UTILITY DISCOUNTING

Experimental evidence from psychology and behavioral economics has identified a number of ways individuals make choices inconsistent with exponential discounting (Frederick et al. 2002; Chabris et al. 2008). The findings of a survey experiment by Thaler (1981) nicely illustrate three of the inconsistencies. First, and most directly challenging exponential discounting, he finds support for the hypothesis "that the discount rate implicit in choices will vary inversely with the length of time to be waited" (p. 202). His simple illustration very effectively motivates this hypothesis: it is quite plausible that someone might choose receiving one apple immediately rather than two apples tomorrow but choose two apples one year plus one day from now over one apple one year from now. The amounts of money respondents would have to receive at various future times to make them indifferent between an immediate payment of some amount and waiting for the larger payment generally show the predicted lower discount rates for payments further in the future.

Second, consistent with research on self-control, he also found support for the hypothesis "that the discount rate will vary inversely with the size of the reward [increase in payment] for which the individual must wait" (Thaler 1981, 202). Motiving this hypothesis is a model of impatience in which waiting for a reward requires mental effort that does not increase with the size of the reward, making it more likely that an individual will find the reward larger than the required mental effort. Again, increases in the amount of the immediate payment generally result in rewards implying lower discount rates.

Third, he tested the hypothesis that individuals treat losses and gains differently. Exponential discounting requires that individuals be willing to pay the same amount to accelerate a gain of, say, $100 dollars by one month as they are to delay a loss of $100 by one month. Respondents employed lower discount rates for losses than for comparable gains. Although respondents displayed an inverse relationship between the discount rate and the size of loss, they did not show the declining discount rate for payments further in the future found for gains. The different treatment of gains and losses is consistent with the type of valuation function used in prospect theory introduced in Chapter 4.

Psychologists, drawing on experimental evidence from both animals and humans, often model time or "delay" discounting with a hyperbolic rather than an exponential function (Ainslie 1975). The functional form for the hyperbolic discount factor is

$$H_T = 1/(1 + \rho T) \qquad \text{(EQ. 6.3)}$$

where H_T is the discount factor T periods in the future and ρ is the individual's discount rate. Figure 6.2 displays exponential and hyperbolic discounting factors calibrated to be equal at 20 periods. The exponential discount factors for the time periods, shown by the solid line, are based on a discount rate, d = 0.05 per period. The hyperbolic discount factors, shown by the dashed line, are based on a discount rate, ρ = 0.08 per period. Relative to the exponential discounting, the hyperbolic discounting shows greater impatience (relatively smaller discount factors) in considering outcomes in the near future, but the relative impatience eventually declines as outcomes closer to 20 periods are considered. Beyond 20 periods the relationship reverses, with the hyperbolic discount factors become larger than the exponential discount factors.

An alternative discounting function that sharpens the distinction between the very short-run and subsequent periods is quasi-hyperbolic, a functional form that Phelps and Pollak (1968) introduced to the economics literature in their modeling of optimal growth when the current generation views future generations with less than perfect altruism. It became common in the behavioral economics literature following its use by Laibson (1997) to explain how less than perfect liquidity of assets may provide an opportunity for individuals with temporally inconsistent preferences to commit to more rational decisions. Quasi-hyperbolic discount factors have the following form:

$$QH_T = \beta\delta^T \qquad \text{(Eq. 6.4)}$$

where $T \geq 1$ is the number of periods beyond the present, $0<\beta<1$ captures the degree of immediate impatience (a smaller β shows greater impatience), and $\delta = 1/(1+d_q)$ depends on a discount rate d_q per period. The dotted line in Figure 6.2 shows the quasi-hyperbolic discount factors for $\beta = 0.8$ and $\delta = 0.9634$ ($d_q = .038$), which calibrates it to equal the exponential and hyperbolic discount factors at 20 periods in the future. After the large initial drop, the quasi-hyperbolic discount factors decline at a slower rate than the exponential discount factors. A person whose utility

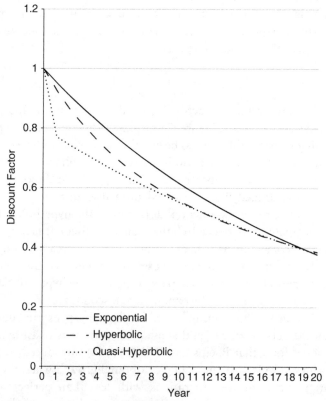

Motivated by Chabris et al. (2008), Figure 1.

FIGURE 6.2 Exponential ($d = 0.05$), Hyperbolic ($\rho = 0.08$), and Quasi-Hyperbolic Discounting ($\beta = 0.8$, $\delta = 0.9634$)

is linear in money discounting with these particular quasi-hyperbolic discount factors would choose receiving $100 dollars immediately over receiving $125 next period. However, looking forward beyond the current period to some future period T, the person would always choose to wait to obtain the $25 increase in payment in period T+1. However, the future choice to wait for the reward is dynamically inconsistent in the sense that when the person actually reaches period T, impatience would lead to the choice to forgo the reward in favor of immediate payment.

Although hyperbolic and quasi-hyperbolic discounting continue to be widely accepted in behavioral research, critics have argued that, when held to the same empirical standards as exponential discounting, they also can be rejected (Rubinstein 2003; Luhmann 2013). Looking across studies, much of the behavioral deviation from exponential discounting disappears when studies involving only delays of less than one year are eliminated (Frederick et al. 2002). Recent research suggests that heuristic models in which individuals compare arguments for and against the available options can outperform the parametric exponential, hyperbolic, or quasi-hyperbolic discounting models to explain short-run intertemporal choices involving delays of less than approximately a month. Ericson et al. (2015) implement a particular heuristic model that outperforms the parametric models by assuming individuals place weights on both the absolute and percentage differences in the money amounts and time differences between alternatives.

Descriptively, behavioral research shows greater impatience in making short-run relative to long-run decisions about trading delay for greater rewards. From the perspective of conventional neoclassical analysis, such time inconsistency is a mistake in the sense that it does not maximize the present value of utility. However, as already noted, the parameterization of global utility as the discounted sum of separable period-specific utilities that underlies conventional analysis was advanced by Samuelson (1937) as an expediency rather than a normative claim. From the behavioral perspective, such impatience is a mistake to the extent that it represents a lack of self-control: individuals would consider themselves better off if they were able to prevent themselves from falling prey to their own impatience.

DEFENDING PRESENT VALUES BASED ON EXPONENTIAL DISCOUNTING

Several arguments support the continued use of exponential discounting to convert streams of future net benefits to present values in spite of the behavioral findings of impatience. Robinson and Hammitt (2011) argue that most policies compared in CBA have time horizons much longer than those over which impatience manifests in behavioral studies. They also suggest that impatient behavior may not be the result of thoughtful consideration and therefore it may be inconsistent with the goal of providing lasting improvements in welfare. Further, they note that underlying discounting is social opportunity cost as well as time preference, and that behavioral research applies only to the latter.

Another line of argument recognizes that imperfections in capital markets "even out" in the absence of impatience. Estimates of the marginal rate of pure time preference are usually based on the long-run rate of return on government bonds (Moore et al. 2004). The willingness of consumers to buy these bonds indicates a willingness to forgo immediate for future consumption at this rate. However, people generally cannot borrow at this rate, except by selling bonds already held. Most consumers must borrow through other mechanisms because they have low incomes, illiquid assets, or poor credit histories. For some people, payday loans and increased credit card balances at very high rates of interest may be the only borrowing options available. Impatience may be relevant to the extent of use of these sources of loans, but not to the absence of opportunities to trade future for current consumption at the rate of return on government bonds. On the production side of the market, the assumption that all entrepreneurs can borrow at the rate of return on private investment also assumes an unrealistically efficient capital market. The neoclassical representative consumer, introduced by Ramsey (1928) and consistent with a long-term perspective on economic growth, is attractive because it assumes away these problem of imperfect capital markets.

Putting aside issues of benefit validity, these arguments suggest the following:

PGL 6.1 *Exponential discounting should be used for policies with intra-generational impacts.*

This call for conventional practice parallels that made for the use of evidence-based probability estimates in calculating expected surpluses set out in Chapter 4 in that it is based on a combination of normative argument and expediency. As with the behavioral challenges to the expected utility hypothesis, the more difficult question is the implications of non-exponential discounting by individuals for benefit validity.

NON-EXPONENTIAL DISCOUNTING AND BENEFIT VALIDITY

Although the impatience in the present inherent in non-exponential discounting manifests itself in the very short run, it can result in decisions that cast long shadows into the future. Immediate choices about consumption affect the accumulation of human capital, especially in terms of health and education, physical capital, and financial assets. The threats to benefit validity involving faulty risk perception discussed in Chapter 4 primarily arise from concerns about behaviors that bring into question inferences within the neoclassical framework. In the case of non-exponential discounting, a more fundamental question is whether choices inconsistent with neoclassical assumptions really are mistakes that can be corrected by policy for the benefit of the individual (Viscusi and Gayer 2015).

The question is most difficult to answer for decisions affecting the accumulation of physical capital in the form of durable goods such as appliances and automobiles. Beginning with Hausman (1979) and Gately (1980), economists have imputed individual discount rates from consumer decisions involving tradeoffs between the initial price of capital goods and the streams of future savings from reduced energy use (Newell and Siikamaki 2015). The estimated discount rates are typically high, especially for lower income consumers, and show considerable variation across individuals. High discount rates have been taken as an indication of "behavioral market failures" and used to justify regulations. Indeed, the CBAs supporting recent federal rules promoting more energy efficient vehicles, appliances, and light bulbs predict most of their benefits would result from lower fuel costs for purchasers (Gayer and Viscusi 2013).

Counting the fuel savings as benefits assuming exponential discounting at a single social discount rate can be challenged on a number of grounds. First, Gayer and Viscusi (2013) note that capital goods can have many dimensions of quality relevant to consumers, and different consumers may place different weights on the dimensions. If fuel savings are gained at the expense of other valued dimensions of quality, then they will overestimate the benefits to the individual. There may be additional losses if the savings result from a reduction in the range of choices so that heterogeneous preferences cannot be as fully satisfied. There may also be heterogeneity in the use of goods that make the predicted fuel savings themselves differ substantially across individuals from those predicted in terms of average intensity of use and duration of ownership.

Second, as already noted, people differ in terms of the rate at which they can borrow for current expenditure against future earnings.

Especially low-income consumers may face very high rates, making the purchase price very important. In the absence of consumer credit at lower rates, some consumers may be forced to fund purchases by effectively borrowing against future energy savings by purchasing a less efficient but less expensive appliance or automobile. From this perspective, "under consumption" of the energy efficient versions of these products results not from excessive impatience in the short-run but rather from an incomplete capital market that does not allow all individuals to smooth their intertemporal consumption at the social discount rate to maximize their global utility.

Third, consumers may not have sufficient information or cognitive resources to make choices that best satisfy their preferences. The greater the number of quality dimensions of the good in question and the greater the variance across dimensions, the greater is the likelihood of inefficient choices resulting from information asymmetries between sellers and buyers (Vining and Weimer 1988). That is, if sellers have accurate information about quality, then providing it to buyers would increase their utility by allowing them to make choices that better satisfy their preferences. Efficient choices also require that the potential buyers correctly interpret and actually use the information. Repeated provision of information may be required to change purchasing behaviors—research suggests that consumers continue to respond but do not fully habituate their responses to home energy reports even after several years (Allcott and Rogers 2014). The format of the information may be especially important. For example, something as simple as the fuel efficiency of automobiles can be difficult to interpret. As is often the case with measures involving division, miles per gallon can be an ineffective way of communicating the relative efficiency of vehicles—most consumers would be surprised if shown a calculation that replacing a car that gets 12 mph with one that gets 14 mph reduces the gallons of gasoline needed to travel 100 miles by the same amount as would replacing a car that gets 28 mpg with one that gets 42 mpg (Larrick and Soll 2008). Information asymmetry is one of the canonical market failures within the neoclassical framework. Limited cognition for appropriately interpreting information falls within the behavioral framework, but restricting choice by imposing minimum standards is only one policy instrument for addressing it.

Our limited capacity for predicting supply-side responses in durable goods markets calls for some caution in rejecting policy-induced changes. In particular, economies of scale and scope, as well as innovation, may reduce the incremental costs of standards over the long run relative to those that would have resulted in the absence of the policy. For example, the short-run costs of tighter fuel efficiency standards in the United States appear to be two or three times higher than the long-run costs (Anderson et al. 2011). If long-run costs are sufficiently small, then the induced efficiency may not substantially affect the availability of other attributes desired by consumers. In the extreme case in which innovation allowed the industry to provide the increased efficiency without reducing the availability of other features at the original price, monetized fuel savings would be a valid measure of internal benefits.

Consumer credit instruments can also involve products with complex dimensions, but with sufficient understanding and calculation they may be converted into simpler dimensions over which individuals have preferences, such as monthly payments, total interest costs, or average returns. However, widespread lack of financial literacy hinders many consumers in their efforts to simplify the complexity (Lusardi and Mitchell 2007). Financial mistakes, such as accepting excessive interest rates or high fee payments, appear to be most frequent for young and old, relative to middle-aged, borrowers (Agarwal et al. 2009). Better informing, or otherwise preventing such mistakes, serves as a rationale for the regulation of consumer finance (Campbell et al. 2011).

With respect to consumer durables and credit instruments, information asymmetries and limited cognition appear to explain choices that fully informed and capable consumers would regret and therefore can be unequivocally considered mistakes. In these situations, non-exponential discounting is likely only a secondary factor and unlikely to be a primary justification for rejecting the benefit validity of revealed preferences. Several other types of decisions, however, potentially display regretful choices even when individuals are fully informed. Impatience with respect to education can substantially reduce future earnings (Cadena and Keys 2015). Consumption of harmful addictive substances, the subject of the next chapter, often fits this description. Less dramatic are decisions involving "good habits" such as saving during productive years to smooth consumption during retirement or engaging in regular physical activity to promote health. Are failures to save or exercise regularly clearly mistakes so that their policy-induced avoidance produces benefits?

Perhaps the most notable policy implication from behavioral economics is the differential impact of opt-in versus opt-out program participation, which, because the transaction costs of opting in or out are comparable, would not be predicted by the neoclassical model. For example, company-sponsored savings plans appear to have much higher participation rates when new employees must make an explicit decision not to join the plans (opt-out) than having to make an explicit decision to join them (opt-in) because of cognitive burden, inertia, or the interpretation of the default option as investment advice (Madrian and Shea 2001, Beshears et al. 2009). Is the influence of the framing of the decision to save as opt-out rather than opt-in an ancillary condition irrelevant to welfare? As many employees appear not to make optimal savings decisions as predicted by life-cycle models, because of procrastination or lack of self-control as captured in hyperbolic discounting, an argument can be made that adopting opt-out nudges people to make welfare-enhancing decisions (Thaler and Benartzi 2004). However, again because of heterogeneity in preferences and opportunities, increased participation resulting from inertia or lack of mental effort could instead be welfare reducing if it results in some individuals saving too much. More generally, the optimal participation rates relevant to welfare analysis depend on the use of alternative behavioral models of opt-out costs, procrastination, inattention, and psychological anchoring (Bernheim et al. 2015).

The implications of present-biased preferences depend on whether people are either sophisticated or naïve about their self-control in the future. O'Donoghue and Rabin (1999) define people as sophisticated if they foresee that they will face self-control problems in the future and naïve if they do not. They consider the decision about when to engage in a one-time activity involving either immediate cost or immediate benefit. In their model, the naïve suffer harm from inappropriately delaying the immediately costly activity and the sophisticated suffer harm from not delaying the immediately rewarding activity when it should be delayed. For example, the results of an experiment in which the treatment was a $100 payment to attend a gym eight times in one month found that those in both the treatment and control groups greatly over-predicted their future attendance, suggesting that they were naïve with respect to their future self-control (Acland and Levy 2015).

Is there a more general way to assess welfare changes when policies potentially counteract lack of self-control? Faruk Gul and Wolfgang Pesendorfer (2004, 2005) reframe dynamic inconsistency in terms of temptations that are psychologically costly for individuals to control. (See also Fudenberg and Levina 2011). The key feature of their reframing is to shift the perspective from the individual's selection of an alternative with immediate consequences to the prior selection of the choice set from which alternatives will be selected. In contrast to the conventional formulation of rational choice, an individual may choose a proper subset of the choice set over the full choice set so as to avoid temptations in the future. For example, someone seeking to lose weight may prefer a choice set that excludes desirable desserts over one that includes them: if they are available, then the temptation will be strong to consume them, either subjecting the person to the disutility of resisting the temptation or bearing the longer-run costs of succumbing to it.

The switch in perspective to decisions over choice sets provides a potential lever for assessing whether imposed "self-control" improves a person's welfare. Imagine that a company wishes to promote better health among its employees. To do so, it eliminates junk-food vending machines from its offices so that employees cannot conveniently consume junk food on the spur of the moment. Whether this company policy improves the welfare of any particular employee depends on whether that employee would voluntarily choose having no junk-food vending machines over having them. This choice would reveal the individual's preference for the company policy. Gul and Pesendorfer (2004) thus extend revealed preference theory to situations in which individuals potentially seek to reduce the disutility of self-control by limiting their own future choices. Policies that help individuals reduce the disutility of self-control provide a relevant benefit for CBA:

PGL 6.2 *The conceptual basis for assessing benefits from policies that restrict individual choice in response to non-exponential time discounting should be willingness to pay for reductions in the disutility of self-control.*

Unfortunately, there do not appear to be many circumstances in which such revealed preferences can be observed and used in benefit estimation. The contracts individuals choose for goods like credit cards, cell phone services, and gym memberships provide some opportunity in these areas, but it has so far been difficult to distinguish commitment decisions that make temptations less attractive from cognitive errors. For example, a study of membership contracts for health clubs offers commitment as only one of nine possible explanations for consumers choosing contracts that were not financially optimal for their levels of utilization (DellaVigna and Malmendier 2006). With respect to benefit validity in CBA, the difficulties of finding consumer data relevant to public policy alternatives and in identifying willingness to pay for reductions in the disutility of self-control severely limit the opportunity for revealed preference studies. Consequently, predicting the benefits of policies that restrict the choices available to consumers most likely requires stated preference methods:

PGL 6.3 *For policies that restrict consumer choice, stated preference methods should be used to estimate the mean willingness to pay for reductions in the disutility of self-control of the relevant population when revealed preference methods are impractical.*

Investment in stated preference studies would likely be practical only for CBAs of major policy changes. However, general research into the valuation of reductions in the disutility of self-control through population-based stated preference studies might produce plausible rules-of-thumb to guide analysts when policy-specific studies are impractical.

These practical guidelines addressing benefit validity reflect a shift in emphasis away from characterizing individuals' time discounting over long periods as hyperbolic, quasi-hyperbolic, or otherwise non-exponential to characterizing it in terms of temptation and the disutility of self-control. The next chapter addresses a particularly pernicious source of temptation: addiction resulting from prior consumption.

CONCLUSION

Although considerable debate continues over the appropriate social discount rate, exponential discounting, at least for intragenerational policies, remains unquestioned in conventional CBA. It is consistent with the workings of capital markets with respect to the trading of resources over time and it is the only discounting function that guarantees dynamic consistency in choices. However, assuming that individuals have a global utility that can be expressed as the sum of exponentially discounted future-period utilities is a strong assumption that appears often violated by the display of impatience in immediate choices. If predictions of costs and benefits are valid, its violation does not invalidate the use of exponential discounting in determining present values. However, non-exponential discounting may be relevant to benefit validity. In particular, an individual may have a willingness to pay for policies that reduce the disutility of self-control in responding to immediate temptations. The key to integrating the behavioral findings about time preference into CBA lies in finding ways to measure this willingness to pay.

7

Harmful Addictive Consumption

Our current consumption of a good can affect our future demand for it. Through the experience of consumption, we may develop a taste or distaste for the good, which leads us to either seek it out or avoid it. Or we may simply develop habits that lead us to repeat a prior consumption choice without having to invest any cognitive effort in considering alternatives. Although these psychological processes require modification of the neoclassical model of consumer choice, they can to some extent be accommodated within it—the former by models of rational addiction and the latter by taking account of the costs of cognition. Individuals whose consumption has been shaped by these processes would neither generally be dissatisfied with their consequences nor wish not to follow them. However, prior consumption leads some people to make repeated consumption choices that they subsequently, or even contemporaneously, regret. In common parlance, we would say these people are addicted to the consumption. Such harmful addictions bring into question revealed preferences as the basis for measuring benefits in CBA.

Perceptions of addiction, which have ranged from moral weakness to brain disease, affect the extent to which it is treated primarily as either a criminal justice or a medical problem. Neuroscience research findings that consumption of substances commonly thought of as addictive change the structure and functioning of the brain prompted calls for addiction to be considered a brain disease (Leshner 1997; Volkow and Li 2004). The definition adopted by the American Society of Addiction Medicine in 2011 heeded these calls: "Addiction is a primary, chronic disease of brain reward, motivation, memory and related circuitry. Dysfunction in these circuits leads to characteristic biological, psychological, social and spiritual manifestations. This is reflected in an individual pathologically pursuing reward and/or [sic] relief by substance use and other behaviors" (ASAM 2016, 1; Smith 2012, 3). It includes not only chemical or substance addictions, such as to alcohol, illicit drugs, and tobacco, but also compulsive or behavioral addictions, such as to gambling, sex, or internet use. The observation of "addiction hopping," by which individuals switch to a new expression of addiction when an old one is blocked, suggests that a more general disease of addiction may underlie any particular manifestation (Richter and Foster 2014); so too do similarities in neurological processes associated with addiction (Goodman 2008).

Accepting this definition would help clarify addictive consumption for purposes of CBA by allowing analysts to treat it as they would self-harmful behaviors resulting from mental illness; that is, not as a manifestation of true preferences. However, the definition of addiction as a brain disease is not universally accepted. Critics point to growing evidence of substantial neuroplasticity throughout life, arguing that any repeated behavior can change brain structure and function (Hall et al. 2015; Lewis 2015). Changes in neural function must be sufficient to cause impairment for it to be considered a disease, which is not always the case (Levy 2013, 3389): "addiction is not a brain disease (though it is often a disease, and it may always involve brain dysfunction)." Neuroplasticity also suggests that, unlike some other chronic diseases, it may be possible to reverse addiction through either abstinence or the repetition of behaviors less harmful than the addiction.

Another reason the medical definition does not clarify addiction sufficiently for CBA is the heterogeneous responses of individuals to potentially addictive substances and behaviors. Most adults can comfortably consume moderate amounts of alcohol with meals, possibly even benefiting their health, but some face a high risk of an initial drink leading immediately to many more drinks and drunkenness, with adverse health, safety, and social consequences. Most adults can recreationally gamble, expecting on average small losses that are effectively the price for this form of recreation, but so-called problem gamblers almost inevitably immiserate themselves, causing harm to themselves and their families. In each of these cases, most people make reasoned decisions about consumption of the potentially addictive good just as they do for the other goods they consume so that their choices fit within the neoclassical paradigm. Those who display addiction, however, do not. Markets for the potentially addictive goods aggregate both types of consumption, complicating immensely the task of making inferences about consumer benefit from revealed preferences.

Although relatively small fractions of consumers of substances widely regarded as addictive actually consume addictively, their consumption is nonetheless costly to society. In the United States, tobacco, illicit drugs, and alcohol consumption impose more than $600 billion annually in productivity, health, and crime-related costs (US NIDA 2012). The fraction of these costs borne internally by the consumer or externally by others varies substantially. Illicit drug and alcohol consumption impose large external costs, while tobacco use imposes most of its costs on the smokers and chewers themselves. CBA treats reductions in external costs unequivocally as benefits. The proper treatment of reductions in internal costs net of any utility losses from reduced consumption is less clear. On the one hand, the demand for products and services to help reduce consumption of goods such as tobacco and alcohol, so-called anti-markets (Winston 1980), suggests that individuals themselves can receive benefits from policies that reduce their consumption of addictive goods. On the other hand, not everyone expresses such demands, making the benefits of induced reductions in their consumption less clear. Assessing these benefits requires an explanation of addiction within an economic framework.

In this chapter, we begin by sketching the model that places addiction within the neoclassical framework: the theory of rational addiction, which has had a prominent place in the economic literature on consumer choice. We then consider several of the explanations of addiction provided by behavioral economics (Bickel and Marsch 2001; Vuchinich and Heather 2003; Redish et al. 2008; Bickel et al. 2014), including those related to delay discounting and the psychic costs of self-control introduced in the last chapter as well as cue-triggered mistakes that result in addictive consumption (Laibson 2001; Bernheim and Rangel 2004). As in previous chapters, we consider the implications of the behavioral explanations for the benefit validity of revealed preferences.

RATIONAL ADDICTION

The neoclassical framing of addiction preserves consumer rationality: the individual chooses current consumption to maximize global utility, which, as discussed in Chapter 6, can be written as the exponentially discounted sum of utilities in the current and future periods. Borrowing an approach from growth models with intertemporally dependent preferences (Ryder and Heal 1973), addiction is captured by allowing the utility in any period to be a function of past as well as current consumption, relaxing BERA3 set out in Chapter 2. Past consumption accumulates, typically with depreciation, into a stock of the addictive good that enters as an argument, like current consumption, in a stable utility function that has a value in any period depending only on its arguments.

In simplest form, intertemporally dependent preferences can be written such that an individual's period-specific utility at some time τ is

$$U_\tau = u(x_\tau, s_\tau, S_\tau) \qquad \text{(EQ. 7.1)}$$

where x_τ is a vector of non-addictive goods consumed, s_τ is the quantity of the addictive good consumed, and S_τ is the accumulated stock of the addictive good. Note that the function, u, is stable in that it is not subscripted for time. S_τ is a function of the quantities of the addictive good consumed in prior periods. An example of a particular function for S_τ is

$$S_\tau = S_{\tau-1} + s_\tau - dS_{\tau-1} \qquad \text{(EQ. 7.2)}$$

where d is the rate at which the stock depreciates.

The desire to show that unusual consumption behavior, like that of addictive goods, could be understood without abandoning the assumption of stable preferences was a motivation for the model of addiction presented by Stigler and Becker (1977). They introduce the concept of consumption capital (S_τ in Equation 7.1), which depends in some way on experience with the good. Differences in age, education, and consumptive experience create different price elasticities of demand across individuals who nonetheless have identically stable preferences. With respect to addiction, consumption is potentially beneficial if it increases consumption capital and potentially harmful if it decreases consumption capital. Their example of beneficial addiction, music appreciation, involves accumulation of consumption capital through past consumption of music; their example of harmful addiction, heroin use, involves reductions in consumption capital for producing euphoria resulting from past consumption of heroin. Within this framework of beneficial consumption increasing consumption capital and harmful consumption reducing it, whether beneficial or harmful addiction actually occurs depends primarily on the price elasticity of demand for the good: "a high elasticity suggests harmful and a low elasticity suggests beneficial addiction" (Stigler and Becker 1977, 81)—later analysis showed the relevant elasticity to be more intertemporally complicated than current own-price elasticity (Boyer 1983; Iannaccone 1986). Nonetheless, it is quite possible that, within this framework, individuals could maximize global utility by making contemporary choices that put them on life-paths involving alcoholism or nicotine addiction. Absent externalities from consumption of the good, it would not be possible for public policy to increase welfare unless it changed the way the addictive good contributes to consumption capital.

The subsequent, and more widely recognized, model of rational addiction was set out in Becker and Murphy (1988). It extends the earlier model in a number of ways. First, potentially addictive goods can have effects on both future earnings and the utility of future consumption. Second, rationality involves choosing a consistent plan for utility maximization over time, requiring more sophisticated analytical approaches that generally allow for multiple steady-state solutions. Third, the stock of the addictive good can be endogenously depreciated, through either purposeful abstention (choosing $s_\tau = 0$) or expenditures on anti-market goods that reduce it and could be represented by an additional negative term in Equation 7.2. Fourth, short term exogenous shocks of anxiety or tension can induce an addictive response.

Addiction within this model requires a large effect of past consumption on current consumption (i.e., strong complementarity of consumption in different time periods). In such cases, steady-state consumption levels tend to be unstable, so that small deviations from the optimal path tend to result in shifts to new steady states with either very low levels of consumption (abstention) or very high levels of consumption (stereotypical addiction). The latter, in turn, may induce endogenous depreciation, thus yielding a pattern of binges in consumption followed by efforts to go "cold turkey." Within the context of exponential discounting, the higher the discount rate, the weaker the complementarity of current and future consumption required to produce addiction. Changes in current, but more so permanent, prices affect the degree of addiction. Changes in life circumstances, such as divorce or death of a spouse, that lower utility and increase the marginal utility of consumption of the addictive good can have the same effect as price changes. Thus, a change in circumstance could trigger addictive consumption.

Empirical tests of rational addiction have generally relied on aggregate time series data to detect the predicted intertemporal relationship of the consumption of possibly addictive goods, such as cigarettes (Becker et al. 1994). However, the ubiquitous autocorrelation in consumption data found in aggregate time series for almost any good biases tests toward acceptance of the rational addiction model (Auld and Grootendorst 2004). Nonetheless, the model has been used as the basis for assessing the social costs of alternative policy interventions to deal with addictive goods such as illicit drugs (Clarke and Byford 2009). A survey of economists who published English-language research related to rational addiction in journals before 2010 reported that a majority of respondents thought that its use is an "academic success story" but were more divided over its empirical support and welfare implications (Melberg and Rogeberg 2010, 8).

BEHAVIORAL EXPLANATIONS

Although the rational addiction model can produce patterns of consumption consistent with common perceptions of addiction, it does so through either exogenous shocks involving stress or small deviations from the optimal path when there is strong complementarity of consumption across time periods. The latter are clearly mistakes. Behavioral economics provides several explanations for such mistakes: misperception of risk, non-exponential discounting, cue-triggered consumption, and costly self-control.

Misperception of Risk. As discussed in Chapter 4, considerable evidence has accumulated suggesting that people have difficulty assessing and using probabilities in situations involving risk. The failure of people to assess correctly either the risk that current consumption poses for future addiction or the probabilities or magnitudes of adverse consequences from that addiction could put them on addictive paths. From the perspective of epidemiological models of drug abuse that see the drug-using peer as the disease vector (Kozel and Adams 1986), potential abusers may assess risks from observing other new users who are enjoying euphoria without manifesting the adverse effects from long-term use. Misperception may also be a factor in addiction to prescription drugs because of the sense of safety conveyed by their medical use (Compton and Volkow 2006). Failure to take account of risks is also a potential explanation for the initiation of addictive consumption during adolescence, a common time for the start of addictive consumption of alcohol, tobacco, and recreational drugs, though as discussed in the next section, impulsive behavior seems to be a more empirically grounded explanation.

Some researchers assess the welfare implications of addictive consumption by treating it like an informational asymmetry in which individuals' demands overestimate their marginal valuations because they underestimate their own future risks. For example, in the case of cigarette smoking, policies that reduce smoking yield benefits to the smokers themselves by reducing the amount of consumption for which marginal valuation falls below price (Jin et al. 2015). Although such information asymmetry was plausible for adults in the last century, it does not seem so now. Indeed, even by the mid-1980s it appears that both smokers and nonsmokers on average overestimated the risk of lung cancer from smoking (Viscusi 1990). Smokers appear not to underestimate the total mortality risks or loss of longevity from smoking (Viscusi 2002). Based on the analysis of data from four waves of the US Health and Retirement Survey, Smith and colleagues (2001) found that the longevity estimates of both smokers and nonsmokers were predictive of their actual mortality. However, it does appear that older adult smokers do have a number of misperceptions that may reduce their motivation to quit smoking (Sloan et al. 2003): until they have an adverse health event, such as a heart attack, stroke, or diagnosis of lung cancer, many smokers believe that their personal risks of harm are lower than average; they tend to underestimate the poor quality of life preceding death from smoking-related diseases; and, influenced by public health announcements suggesting that it is never too late to quit, they anticipate being able to quit in the future to begin to reverse the ill effects of smoking. Overall, it appears that misperception of smoking risks does contribute to consumption beyond that which would occur if people accurately anticipated the probabilities and consequences of all health risks. However, the difficulty many smokers face in carrying out their intentions to quit suggest that misperception of risk is far from a complete explanation.

Non-Exponential Discounting and Internalities. The most widely discussed behavioral explanations for addictive consumption involve time inconsistency (Monterosso et al. 2012; Bickel et al. 2014). As discussed in Chapter 6, people often display higher discount rates for delaying immediate consumption than they do for a comparable delay of consumption in the more distant future. Efforts to model this present-bias have replaced the exponential, and uniquely time consistent, discounting of neoclassical economics with hyperbolic or quasi-hyperbolic discounting. In the context of addictive consumption, such non-exponential discounting can be interpreted as individuals imposing future costs on themselves through their impatience. Analogous to one person imposing external costs, or externalities, on another person, a present self can be thought of as imposing internal costs, or internalities, on a future self (Herrnstein et al. 1993). Within this framing, public policies that alter addictive consumption have the potential to provide benefits by reducing the magnitude of internalities.

Gruber and Köszegi (2001) explore the welfare implications of time inconsistency by reformulating the rational addiction model to allow individuals to employ quasi-hyperbolic discounting, as displayed in Equation 6.4: $QH_T = \beta\delta^T$. They find the optimal consumption paths for both naïve individuals (who fail to anticipate that future selves will discount as they do) and sophisticated individuals (who do anticipate that future selves will discount as they do). The rational addiction results of Becker and Murphy (1988) are a special case of their model for sophisticated individuals when discounting is actually exponential without present-bias ($\beta = 1$ in Equation 6.4). Welfare analysis treats the different selves as if they were different individuals realizing benefits at different times. Consistent with standard CBA practice, these amounts are discounted exponentially. Thus, unlike the implications of the rational addiction model, it is possible for policy to increase the present value of benefits by pushing the individual's consumption path closer to that of a sophisticated exponential discounter.

It is worth noting that the quasi-hyperbolic model for sophisticated individuals produces predictions about the price elasticity of demand for the addictive good similar to those of the rational addiction model, making it difficult to derive empirical tests based on market data to distinguish between the models. However, a number of studies find a relationship between discounting and the status of smoking. For example, Ida (2014) finds that under the assumption of quasi-hyperbolic discounting, respondents with greater time discounting (smaller δ) and larger present-bias (smaller β) were more likely to be smokers; further, larger present bias predicted more intensive smoking. Present-bias also appears to help explain both obesity and excessive alcohol consumption (Richards and Hamilton 2012).

Cue-Triggered Consumption. Evidence that environmental cues can trigger behavior stretches from the Pavlovian dogs through experiments on consumer choice (Bushong et al. 2010) to functional magnetic resonance imaging (fMRI) of brain processes associated with addictive consumption (Courtney et al. 2016). When a cue is repeatedly geminated with consumption of a good, the marginal utility from immediate consumption of the good may become higher in the presence of the cue. Most of us feel increased desire for favored foods in the presence of their aromas. Cues, such as open cigarette packs, may simply signal availability. They may trigger the anticipation of pleasure, as an alcoholic drink does for a cigarette or the locale of past euphoria does for an opiate, or as the anticipation of relief from unpleasant feelings, such as from cigarettes or opiates, does in response to stress. Incorporating cues into consumer theory provides explanations for both addiction and effective marketing (Laibson 2001). It also provides an explanation for present-bias by allowing consumer choices to respond immediately to encountered cues.

Bernheim and Rangel (2004) provide the most fully developed application of cue-triggered consumption models to addiction. Individuals are assumed to make decisions about current consumption of the addictive substance using a hedonic forecasting mechanism, M, that depends on a lifestyle activity, a, the stock of prior consumption, S, and a randomly drawn exogenous state of nature, ω:

$$M[C(a, \omega), S, a, \omega] \qquad \text{(EQ. 7.3)}$$

where C measures the intensity of exposure to the substance-related cue as a function of the lifestyle activity and the state of nature.

The possible lifestyle activities in their model are exposure (E), avoidance (A), or rehabilitation (R). E is more intrinsically enjoyable than A and A is more intrinsically enjoyable than R, but E more positively affects cue intensity than A, and A more positively affects cue intensity than R. In addition, R completely blocks current consumption of the substance. Other things equal, M is larger for E than A, and for A than R. Also, M is increasing in C and S. That is, M is larger, the more intense the cue and the greater the level of addiction, as represented by the stock of consumption.

Each individual has some threshold, M^T, such that if, after choosing a lifestyle activity, M is less than M^T, then the individual enters the "cold" decision mode and rationally assesses the implications of current consumption on the exponentially discounted present value of utility. This rational decision may or may not involve consumption of the addictive good. However, if M is greater than or equal to M^T, then the individual enters the "hot" decision mode and consumes the addictive substance, whether or not it maximizes the present value of utility. In terms of the distinction between decision utility and experience utility introduced in Chapter 3, M produces forecasting errors when it exceeds the threshold that switches the individual to the hot mode. It also produces apparent deviations from exponential discounting that would appear as present-bias.

The parameters in the model capture characteristics of the individual through the form of the hedonic forecasting mechanism, M, and the value of the threshold for the hot decision mode, M^T, the nature of the substance through the immediate hedonic payoff from consumption and the effect of past consumption, S, on M, and the environment through its effect on the intensity of cues relevant to the substance. These features allow the modeling approach to predict a number of patterns of behavior consistent with observations of addictive consumption: unsuccessful attempts to quit, cue-triggered recidivism, self-described mistakes, self-control through pre-commitment, and self-control through behavioral therapy. Further, more addictive substances discourage new users (those with $S = 0$ in the current and past periods), but reinforce severe addiction.

Welfare analysis in the context of this model takes individual wellbeing as the sum of exponentially discounted experienced utilities over time periods. Because individuals sometimes make mistakes in the hot decision mode by consuming the addictive good when they would not have done so in the cold decision mode, it is possible for public policy to increase the individual's wellbeing. In other words, it is possible for public policy to produce benefits from induced changes in consumption in the absence of externalities of consumption or production. In addition to policies that have their effect by changing relative prices (taxes and subsidies) or quantities (restrictions on circumstances of use or outright prohibitions) of the addictive substance, policies that affect the intensity of cues, such as graphic warnings on cigarette packages, or changes in the relative prices of rehabilitation services, may also improve welfare. Assessment is complicated, however, because assumptions about parameters can substantially affect optimal policy, perhaps switching the sign of an optimal tax. Further, because parameters depend on the individual as well as the substance and the environment, there is likely to be heterogeneity in terms of whether a general policy imposes benefits or costs on individuals.

Temptation and Costly Self-Control. Chapter 6 introduced Gul and Pesendorfer's (2004) framing of temptation and costly control as an explanation for present-bias. They employ this general approach to assessing the welfare effects of policies directed at harmful addiction by assuming that current consumption increases the future costs of self-control (Gul and Pesendorfer 2007). They define compulsive consumption as occurring if, when faced with a temptation, consumption differs from the consumption choice that would have been made if commitment that blocked the temptation were possible. Addiction makes individuals more compulsive, and it is harmful if it increases divergence between actual choices and those that would have been made in the absence of the temptation. As in their general analysis of temptation, policies that reduce the disutility of self-control provide a benefit to individuals. So too do policies that facilitate commitment to avoiding future temptation.

Framing of addiction in terms of temptation and costly self-control helps explain why many addictions begin with consumption during adolescence. For example, nearly 90 percent of US adult smokers tried their first cigarette before the age of 18 years (US CDC 2016), and "loss of autonomy" over tobacco use can occur in very young adolescents within days of first inhaling from a cigarette (DiFranza et al. 2007). Adolescents who begin drinking alcohol before the age of 15 are six times more likely to develop alcohol dependence during adulthood than those who begin drinking after the age of 21 years (US SAMHSA 2014). Major changes in brain structure and processes occur at the onset of puberty. These changes manifest as greater adolescent risk taking, impulsive choice, sensation seeking, novelty preference, and reward preference compared to adults, but also to less inhibitory control than adults (Johnson et al. 2009; Sturman and Moghaddam 2011).

Once engaged in addictive consumption, adults often do find self-control costly and therefore face difficulties in avoiding temptation. For example, in a 2011 survey, nearly 70 percent of US adult smokers expressed a desire to stop smoking, and more than 40 percent reported having attempted to quit during the past year (US DHHS 2014). Not only is quitting smoking difficult, but many smokers relapse after successful quits—over 35 percent of British smokers who successfully quit for at least a year relapsed within the following ten years (Hawkins et al. 2010). It also appears that for some addictive substances, such as opioids, individuals underestimate the costs of self-control in the face of temptation when they are not actually being tempted (Badger et al. 2007). Further, the large expenditures individuals make in anti-markets, such as those for smoking and obesity, are consistent with them valuing commitment against temptations. So too is the dramatic rise in support in the United States for restrictions on smoking in public places from smokers as well as nonsmokers (Hersch 2005).

SUMMARY

In contrast to the model of rational addiction, the behavioral models of addiction allow individuals to make mistakes in the sense of making consumption choices that are not in their own long-term interests. Although misperception of risk and quasi-hyperbolic discounting have some plausibility and empirical support, the models that interpret present-bias in terms of cue-triggered consumption or temptation with costly self-control better explain the particular patterns of consumption commonly associated with addiction and provide clear bases for welfare analysis. Defining harmful addiction as do Gul and Pesendorfer (2007), the behavioral models of addiction suggest the following practical guideline:

PGL 7.1 *Policies that reduce harmful addictive consumption or its adverse consequences for the harmfully addicted provide internal benefits to them.*

Unfortunately, this guideline is conditional on the specific substance or behavior being assessed, the particular environment in which choices about it are made, and the individual making the choice—the what, when, where, and who of addictive consumption cannot be fully separated. The guideline applies directly only to policies that affect only the addicted. For example, an intervention that reduced cigarette consumption by smokers who could reasonably be assumed to be addicted to tobacco because they sought assistance in quitting would provide internal benefits to participants measured in terms of reduced health risks and avoided expenditures. However, its application to market data requires recognition that the demand for potentially addictive goods comes from both those who are addicted to the good and those who are not. Unless those who are not addicted miscalculate the risks of adverse consequences, inducing reductions in their consumption is not necessarily welfare improving. Dealing with this heterogeneity, which is unique to each potentially addictive good, requires a framework for interpreting observed market behavior.

Nonetheless, one demographic group stands out as particularly vulnerable to addiction: adolescents. As previously noted, most substance addictions begin with consumption during adolescence. Further, the vulnerability to initiating harmful addiction during adolescence has a strong basis in neuroscience. The great risk of initiation during adolescence suggests:

PGL 7.2 *Reductions in consumption by adolescents of goods that potentially result in harmful addiction provide internal benefits.*

ADDRESSING MARKET HETEROGENEITY: DIVERGENCE BETWEEN DEMAND AND MARGINAL VALUATION

Neoclassical CBA assumes that market demand schedules reveal consumers' marginal valuations of consumption. The line labeled D_M in Figure 7.1 indicates the market demand schedule for a good, which

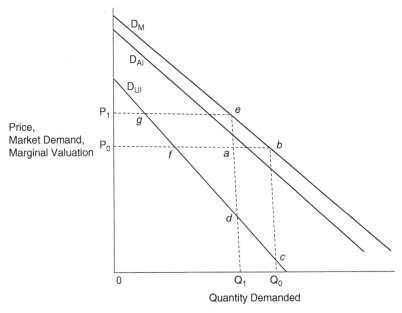

FIGURE 7.1 Benefits from Reductions in Consumption of Harmfully Addictive Goods

could be estimated with sufficient exogenous variation in price over time or across jurisdictions. If consumers are fully informed about the quality of the good, then the height of the schedule above any quantity would indicate consumers' marginal valuation of consumption at that quantity; that is, how much they would value consumption of an additional unit of the good. Further, if consumption does not involve any externalities, then this marginal valuation for individuals would also be the social marginal valuation at that level of consumption. A market demand schedule under these conditions would provide an appropriate basis for measuring the social costs and benefits of changes in prices and quantities for the good.

In some situations individuals do not accurately assess the qualities of a good, either because they do not have relevant information or because they make mistakes in using the information. In the case of missing information, if either producers or third-parties could fully inform them about quality, then the well-recognized market failure of information asymmetry results (Vining and Weimer 1988). In Figure 7.1, an information asymmetry at each quantity is represented by the vertical distance between the uninformed market demand schedule, D_M, and the demand schedule that would result if all consumers were fully informed, D_{AI}. Making information available would reduce demand to D_{AI} only if consumers can use it without error, say in correctly assessing probabilities about their own likelihood of being able to stop consumption of the good in the future when they have an intention to do so. As already noted, some analysts assume that information asymmetry provides a rationale for policies that reduce harmful addictive consumption (Jin et al. 2015; also, see Cutler et al. 2015, who model information asymmetry about cigarettes as an underestimation of the full price of smoking). Although this framing is attractive because it allows analysts to treat addiction as a well-understood market failure, it neither takes account of the more plausible behavioral explanations for addiction nor seems consistent with the rather abundant information most adults have about the risks of the adverse consequences from consumption of potentially addictive goods such as alcohol, tobacco, common recreational drugs, and gambling.

Rather than framing harmful addiction primarily as an information asymmetry problem, it can be modeled as its own market failure. The first conceptual step along this path was provided by the Australia Productivity Commission in its analysis of gambling (APC 1999). It distinguished between the market demand for gambling, which includes demand by so-called problem gamblers, whose consumption fits the definition of harmful addiction, as well as demand by the more numerous recreational gamblers, who consume gambling like other leisure goods. The analysts make the normative assumption that only recreational gamblers receive value from their gambling activity, an assumption that is consistent with problem gamblers compulsively gambling until they have used up their available resources.

The distinction between addictive and unaddictive consumption need not be made in terms of individuals. An addicted individual may have demand resulting from the addiction but may also have demand, and positive marginal valuation, for consumption of the good in the absence of the addiction. For example, much of the cigarette consumption of regular adult smokers can be reasonably attributed to nicotine addiction; nonetheless, these same individuals would derive pleasure from smoking in some situations even if they were not addicted. Thus, the approach of the Productivity Commission can be reinterpreted in terms of the market demand including both addicted and unaddicted consumption, but positive marginal valuation resulting only from the unaddicted consumption. This is the general approach taken by Laux (2000), who proposed treating adolescent consumption of cigarettes as imposing a negative externality on future adult selves (a negative internality). Weimer et al. (2009) and Ashley et al. (2015) also take this approach to assess the benefits of smoking-reduction policies.

Returning to Figure 7.1, D_{UI} represents demand from fully informed and unaddicted consumers. Again, making the normative assumption that only unaddicted demand provides consumer value, it is also the marginal value schedule for valuing changes in consumption. At price P_o the quantity demanded in the market, Q_o, is determined by the market demand schedule, D_M. Imagine a policy, such as a tax or a restriction on the circumstances of use, that raises price from P_o to P_I. Consumption would fall to Q_I. Interpreting the market demand schedule as the marginal valuation schedule, the changes in price and quantity would result in a consumer surplus loss given by the familiar trapezoid bounded by P_I *eb*P_o. But the consumer surplus analysis differs when the unaddicted demand schedule is interpreted as the marginal valuation schedule. In this case, consumers suffer a surplus loss from having to pay more for their remaining consumption, an amount equal to the area of rectangle P_I *ea*P_o. However, because their marginal valuation schedule lies below the market demand schedule, they also enjoy a benefit resulting from the reduction in consumption from Q_o to Q_I because their valuation of these units, equal to the area $Q_I dc Q_o$, was less than the amount they had to pay for them, equal to the area of rectangle $Q_I ab Q_o$, yielding the gain as the area of trapezoid *abdc*. Thus, the net loss of surplus to consumers in this market from the induced price increase is equal to the area P_I *ea*P_o–*abdc*, which, depending on the relative positions of the market and unaddicted demand schedules, could be positive, zero, or negative.

Interpreting unaddicted demand as marginal valuation provides an alternative to accepting either of two extreme approaches to valuing consumer surplus changes in the markets for harmful addictive goods. One extreme approach involves measuring changes in consumer surplus with the conventional assumption that the market demand schedule is also the proper marginal valuation schedule. Another extreme approach, consistent with the prevailing public health perspective on tobacco, involves assuming that reducing the consumption of the goods involves no consumer surplus loss. As noted in Chapter 1, advocates for the latter approach objected to an ad hoc reduction in benefits to take account of the lost consumption value to consumers in the CBA done by Food and Drug Administration analysts of more graphic health warnings in cigarette labeling and advertising (US FDA 2010). Some critics rejected both the neoclassical approach as well as the ad hoc adjustment (Song et al. 2014; Chaloupka et al. 2015). Strong criticism from public health advocates eventually led to the Department of Health and Human Services abandoning its efforts to develop a more firmly grounded method for valuing consumer surplus changes in markets for addictive goods (Begley and Clarke 2015).

Not only should that effort be revived, but it should be based on the following practical guideline:

PGL 7.3 *Policy-induced changes in consumer surplus in the markets for harmful addictive goods should treat the unaddicted demand schedule rather than the market demand schedule as the marginal valuation schedule.*

Some skepticism about the practicality of this guideline is warranted. Although economists routinely estimate market demand schedules using commonly available data, estimating unaddicted demand schedules requires both more assumptions and greater creativity in finding relevant data. Nonetheless, at least two empirical approaches seem possible.

First, people make expenditures in anti-markets to help them overcome addiction or its consequences. Many people spend money on products to help them quit smoking. Others buy diet aids or even have bariatric surgery to help them lose weight. Some even check into rehabilitation centers to help them reduce their alcohol or drug dependence. These behavioral traces provide an opportunity for estimating willingness to pay to eliminate addiction, which in turn may enable analysts to position the unaddicted demand schedule relative to the market demand schedule. Undoubtedly, doing so will require analytical creativity and strong assumptions, especially because not all efforts to avoid addiction are monetized in markets. Nonetheless, executing this sort of revealed preference approach should be a challenge welcomed by economists.

Second, stated preference methods may be useful in more directly estimating the value people place on escaping addiction. For example, Weimer et al. (2009) conducted a contingent valuation survey of a national sample of smokers to elicit willingness to pay for a medication that would completely eliminate the craving for cigarettes for one year. The mean estimates of the willingness to pay across the most plausible estimated models ranged from $311 to $352. Assuming that utility is quadratic in current consumption and the stock of consumption of cigarettes, but separable from other goods, they were able to derive an expression for the ratio of the change in consumer surplus measured using an unaddicted demand schedule to that measured using the market demand schedule as a function of the initial price, the price change, the price elasticity of demand, and the willingness to pay for the elimination of addiction. For a 25 percent price increase and an assumed price elasticity of demand of –0.15, their willingness to pay estimates suggest that about 75 percent of the loss in consumer surplus measured using the market demand schedule should be counted as the lost consumption benefit to consumers from the price increase. This rule of thumb should be used with caution as it is based on a single contingent valuation survey and a specific utility function. However, it demonstrates how stated preference methods can be used to discover unaddicted demand.

In summary, CBAs of policies that reduce harmful addictive consumption reasonably include improvements in health and other aspects of personal wellbeing as internal benefits, but they should also include the lost value of consumption that would have occurred were the good not addictive. Doing so, however, requires an estimate of the demand for the good if it were not addictive.

ILLICIT GOODS

Although many potentially harmful addictive goods, such as alcohol and tobacco, are available in legal markets, many others, such as opiates and most other recreational drugs, are not. Should loss of value from policy-induced reductions in consumption of these illicit goods count as a cost in CBA?

A similar question arose in the early application of CBA to criminal justice policies. Stolen property was a loss to the legal owner but a gain to the thief. Some analysts included the gain to the thief as a benefit that offset to some extent the cost of the loss to the owner (e.g., Long et al. 1981). Other analysts, however, objected that common sense suggests that the benefit to the thief should not count. The issue was eventually framed usefully in terms of the concept of standing—whose costs and benefits should count (Whittington and MacRae 1986). Specifically, Trumbull (1990) argued that criminal gains should not be given standing because they violate absolute legal constraints; just as CBA should take account of physical constraints in assessing benefits, so too should it take account of these legal constraints.

A similar logic can be applied to consumption of illicit goods:

PGL 7.4 *Consumer surplus losses resulting from reductions in the consumption of illicit addictive goods should not be counted as costs in applying CBA to policies that do not change the status of the goods to legal.*

Unlike potentially addictive goods available in legal markets, the internal benefits from avoided adverse effects should be counted in CBA but the costs of lost consumption value should not. The guideline does not apply, however, in applying CBA to legalization or decriminalization policies—these policies expand the consumption with standing. However, the value of the legal or noncriminal consumption that they facilitate should be measured using unaddicted demand schedules.

CONCLUSION

Neuroscience, behavioral economics, and empirical evidence all bring into question the implications of the rational addiction model. By their own reckoning, some people make mistakes by beginning or continuing to consume harmful addictive substances. The addicted confront temptations that lead them to consume to their current or future detriment, most often in terms of reductions in their physical, psychological, financial, or social wellbeing. Policies that reduce the loss of wellbeing provide internal benefits to the harmfully addicted, though these policies also may involve costs in the form of lost consumption value. Taking account of these costs and benefits in CBA is complicated by the substantial heterogeneity in harmful addiction. Some substances are more addictive than others, but, with the possible exception of nicotine consumption by adolescents, most substances can be consumed by most people without leading to harmful addiction. Nonetheless, harmful addiction poses a serious problem for society because some of the addicted impose great harm on themselves or others.

The rapidly advancing field of neuroscience is providing biological foundations for the discovered regularities of behavioral economics generally, as well as their specific application to harmful addiction. It is also likely that advances in neuroscience will lead to behavioral or biological interventions that can directly reduce the costs of self-control that the addicted bear when encountering temptation. Its recognition of neuroplasticity expands harmful addiction from just substances to behaviors by identifying the similarities in the brain changes they produce, but also undercuts the older view that addiction changes the brain in irreversible ways. Consequently, neuroscience is unlikely to resolve soon the challenges that harmful addition poses to CBA.

8

Practical Guidelines for Valuation

CBA based solely on neoclassical economic theory offers conceptual congruence between positive prediction and normative assessment. Its analytical burdens arise primarily from the practical challenges of confidently predicting impacts and applying widely accepted principles to value them. The systematic deviations from the predictions of positive neoclassical economics documented and interpreted by behavioral economists break the neat congruence between the positive and the normative. Were behavioral findings only relevant to prediction, the challenge they pose to CBA would not be of much concern. However, as discussed in the previous chapters, behavioral economics also has implications for valuation that require attention not just to the validity of behavioral predictions but also to the validity of the standard practices for measuring benefits based on neoclassical assumptions.

Laboratory experiments provide the bulk of the empirical evidence on deviations from neoclassical rationality. These experiments enjoy a high degree of internal validity. Their external validity can sometimes be questioned because of the common use of students as subjects and the difference between laboratory and field settings. In particular, markets may mitigate to some extent the consequences of individual irrationality for the sorts of aggregate measures often employed in neoclassical prediction and valuation. Nonetheless, data from a number of field settings confirm the relevance of many of the behavioral predictions. Consequently, the prudent application of revealed preference methods should take account of the possibility of behavioral deviations from rationality. When such deviations appear likely, analysts should acknowledge them and use the growing body of behavioral economics knowledge to assess their possible implications for both prediction and valuation. Chapters 4–7 address the implications of specific deviations from neoclassical rationality for valuation—those related to how risk, time, reference points, and addiction affect people's choices and valuations of consumption.

The development of stated preference methods, particularly contingent valuation, has by necessity been informed by the findings of psychology and behavioral economics—the validity of survey responses depends fundamentally on the cognition of the respondents. Initial concerns about bias from strategic responses soon gave way to more empirically relevant concerns, many voiced by prominent contributors to behavioral economics, about cognitive biases in responses to benefit elicitations. The essential role of stated preference methods for the use of CBA in the assessment of environmental policies initially drove craft improvement to address these concerns. Such improvement is likely to continue as these methods become more commonly used in other policy areas. Some of the practical guidelines offered in previous chapters suggest specific avenues for improvement.

The practical guidelines vary both in terms of breadth and likely acceptance. They begin with a simple reminder that CBA assesses policies in terms of relative efficiencies, something that should be obvious to all policy analysts; yet, it seems not to be so obvious to some scholars suggesting modifications that they see as addressing limitations of CBA as a decision rule. Some guidelines endorse continuing neoclassical practice, as in basing net benefits on expected surplus. Other guidelines suggest changes in common practice, such as no longer avoiding eliciting willingness to accept in contingent valuation when it is the conceptually appropriate benefit measure or basing the measurement of consumption loss on unaddicted demand schedules. Such changes are likely to be controversial.

Of course, I would like to see these guidelines widely accepted and used by policy analysts. However, as they arise from my own current understanding and interpretation of research in behavioral economics, it is likely that some of the guidelines are controversial. As long as controversy draws reasoned argument and relevant research, I will consider my efforts worthwhile.

The following list draws together the practical guidelines from the previous chapters:

PGL 2.1 *CBA assesses only the relative efficiency of policies; values other than efficiency may be relevant to assessing relative social welfare.*

PGL 3.1 *Use whatever theory, behavioral or otherwise, that provides the best predictions of policy impacts.*

PGL 3.2 *In assessing benefits, ignore departures from rationality that do not substantially affect observed behaviors.*

PGL 3.3 *Take advantage of variation in institutional decision rules to help identify relevant ancillary conditions and the range of benefits that they imply.*

PGL 4.1 *Use evidence-based probabilities in expected surplus analyses even when there is reason to believe that they differ from subjective probabilities.*

PGL 4.2 *In benefit transfer from studies involving risk to expected surplus analyses, assess benefit validity by considering the likelihood that individuals irrationally estimate, update, or apply probabilities and the extent to which institutional arrangements mitigate irrationality with respect to the aggregates used in benefit prediction.*

PGL 4.3 *The conduct of stated preference studies involving prospects should communicate probabilities using the best available guidance from the risk communication literature; the assessment of benefit validity in existing studies should consider compliance with risk communication guidance.*

PGL 4.4 *Contingent valuation method surveys in which changes in risks are important features of the goods being valued should include, and results pass, scope tests for a positive relationship between the probabilities of desirable outcomes and willingness to pay.*

PGL 4.5 *Contingent valuation method surveys in which changes in risks are important features of the goods being valued should include questions that allow for the assessment and accommodation of heterogeneity in risk perception and preferences.*

PGL 5.1 *Consistently apply compensating variation using WTP for policies that provide gains to the individual and WTA for policies that impose losses on the individual.*

PGL 5.2 *To preserve the value of CBA in assessing efficiency when extremely large values of WTA dominate net benefits, the sensitivity of net benefits to WTA bounds should be calculated and presented along with estimates of the fractions of the population with values above the bounds.*

PGL 5.3 *Stated preference methods to elicit WTA should employ "incentive-compatible" social budget constraint framings with follow-up questions to assess respondents' perceptions of tradeoffs.*

PGL 6.1 *Exponential discounting should be used for policies with intragenerational impacts.*

PGL 6.2 *The conceptual basis for assessing benefits from policies that restrict individual choice in response to non-exponential time discounting should be willingness to pay for reductions in the disutility of self-control.*

PGL 6.3 *For policies that restrict consumer choice, stated preference methods should be used to estimate the mean willingness to pay for reductions in the disutility of self-control of the relevant population.*

PGL 7.1 *Policies that reduce harmful addictive consumption or its adverse consequences for the harmfully addicted provide internal benefits to them.*

PGL 7.2 *Reductions in consumption by adolescents of goods that potentially result in harmful addiction provide internal benefits.*

PGL 7.3 *Policy-induced changes in consumer surplus in the markets for harmful addictive goods should treat the unaddicted demand schedule rather than the market demand schedule as the marginal valuation schedule.*

PGL 7.4 *Consumer surplus losses resulting from reductions in the consumption of illicit addictive goods should not be counted as costs in applying CBA to policies that do not change the status of the goods to legal.*

Some of the guidelines suggest lines of research that could help improve the application of CBA. Continuing the search for more effective ways to communicate risk information has potential not only for improving stated preference methods, but also for making information policies more effective. Finding ways of improving the use of social budget constraints or introducing other approaches to achieve greater incentive compatibility would increase confidence in the elicitations of willingness to accept when it is the conceptually correct benefit measure. Finding ways to estimate unaddicted demand schedules would allow for better assessment of costs and benefits in markets for harmful addictive substances.

Much of the economics profession was initially skeptical about the behavioral challenges to the neoclassical paradigm; indeed, the original terminology often used—"anomalies"—tended to minimize their importance. As evidence accumulated and became organized as behavioral economics, the profession became more accepting of the importance of apparent deviations from rationality, though largely rejecting the extreme view that the construction of preferences is so contextual as to render them useless as a basis for assessing value. As discussed in Chapter 3, intellectually impressive efforts have sought to integrate behavioral economics into welfare economics. One can hope that eventually these efforts will produce as coherent and applicable a framework for assessing efficiency as that provided by neoclassical welfare economics. In the meantime, however, the analysts charged with actually doing CBA must get on with it. I hope I have provided some help to them. I also hope that more behavioral economists will seek to translate their research into practical advice for these analysts.

References

Acland, Dan (2015) The Case for Ends Paternalism: Extending Le Grand and New's Framework for Justification of Government Paternalism. Working Paper, Goldman School of Public Policy, University of California at Berkeley.

Acland, Dan and Matthew R. Levy (2015) Naiveté, Projection Bias, and Habit Formation in Gym Attendance. *Management Science* 61(1), 146–160.

Adler, Matthew D. (2016) Behavioral Economics, Happiness Surveys, and Public Policy. *Journal of Benefit-Cost Analysis* 7(1), 196–219.

Adler, Matthew D. and Eric A. Posner (1999) Rethinking Cost-Benefit Analysis. *Yale Law Journal* 109(2), 165–247.

Agarwal, Sumit, John C. Driscoll, Xavier Gabaix, and David Laibson (2009) The Age of Reason: Financial Decisions over the Life-Cycle with Implications for Regulation. *Brookings Papers on Economic Activity* (Fall), 51–117.

Ainslie, George (1975) Specious Reward: A Behavioral Theory of Impulsiveness and Impulse Control. *Psychological Bulletin* 82(4), 463–496.

Allais, Par M. (1953) Le Comportement de l'Homme Rationnel devant le Risque: Critique des Postulats et Axiomes de l'Ecole Americaine. *Econometrica* 21(4), 503–546. [English summary included.]

Allcott, Hunt and Todd Rogers (2014) The Short-Run and Long-Run Effects of Behavioral Interventions: Experimental Evidence from Energy Conservation. *American Economic Review* 104(10), 3003–3037.

American Association of Addiction Medicine (2016) Definition of Addiction. www.asam.org/quality-practice/definition-of-addiction.

Anderson, Soren T., Ian W. H. Parry, James M. Sallee, and Carolyn Fischer (2011) Automobile Fuel Economy Standards: Impacts, Efficiency, and Alternatives. *Review of Environmental Economics and Policy* 5(1), 89–108.

Andersson, Henrik (2007) Willingness to Pay for Road Safety and Estimates of the Risk of Death: Evidence from a Swedish Contingent Valuation Study. *Accident Analysis & Prevention* 39(4), 853–865.

Aos, Steve, Marna Miller, and Elizabeth Drake (2006) *Evidence-Based Public Policy Options to Reduce Future Prison Construction, Criminal Justice Costs, and Crime Rates*. Olympia: Washington State Institute for Public Policy.

Arrow, Kenneth J. (1951) *Social Choice and Individual Values*. New York: John Wiley & Sons.

(1964) The Role of Securities in the Optimal Allocation of Risk-Bearing. *Review of Economic Studies* 31(2), 91–96.

Arrow, Kenneth J., Maureen L. Cropper, Christian Gollier, Ben Groom, Geoffrey M. Heal, Richard G. Newell, William D. Nordhaus, Robert S. Pindyck, William A. Pizer, Paul R. Portney, Thomas Sterner, Richard S. J. Tol, and Martin L. Weitzman (2012) How Should Benefits and Costs Be Discounted in an Intergenerational Context? The Views of an Expert Panel. Resources for the Future. Discussion Paper 12–53. December.

Arrow, Kenneth, Robert Solow, Paul Portney, Edward Leamer, Roy Radner, and Howard Schuman (1993) Report of the NOAA Panel on Contingent Valuation. *Federal Register* 58(10), 4601–4614.

Arvidson, Malin, Fergus Lyon, Stephen McKay, and Domenico Moro (2013) Valuing the Social? The Nature and Controversies of Measuring Social Return on Investment (SROI). *Voluntary Sector Review* 4(1), 3–18.

Ashley, Elizabeth M., Clark Nardinelli, and Rosemarie A. Lavaty (2015) Estimating the Benefits of Public Health Policies that Reduce Harmful Consumption. *Health Economics* 24(5), 617–624.

Auld, M. Christopher and Paul Grootendorst (2004) An Empirical Analysis of Milk Addiction. *Journal of Health Economics* 23(6), 1117–1133.

Australia, Productivity Commission (1999) *Australia's Gambling Industries*. Inquiry Report No. 10, 26 November.

(2015) *Productivity Update*. July.

Badger, Gary J., Warren K. Bickel, Louis A. Giordano, Eric A. Jacobs, George Loewenstein, and Lisa Marsch (2007) Altered States: The Impact of Immediate Craving on the Valuation of Current and Future Opioids. *Journal of Health Economics* 26(5), 865–876.

Ballard, Charles L., John B. Shoven, and John Whalley (1985). General Equilibrium Computations of the Marginal Welfare Costs of Taxes in the United States. *American Economic Review* 75(1), 128–138.

Barke, Richard P. and Hank C. Jenkins-Smith (1993) Politics and Scientific Expertise: Scientists, Risk Perception, and Nuclear Waste Policy. *Risk Analysis* 13(4), 425–439.

Bateman, Ian J. and Ian H. Langford (1997) Budget-Constraint, Temporal, and Question-Ordering Effects in Contingent Valuation Studies. *Environment and Planning A* 29(7), 1215–1228.

Bateman, Ian J. and Kenneth G. Willis, Editors. (1999) *Valuing Environmental Preferences: Theory and Practice of the Contingent Valuation Method in the US, EU, and Developing Countries*. New York: Oxford University Press.

Becker, Gary S. and Kevin M. Murphy (1988) A Theory of Rational Addiction. *Journal of Political Economy* 96(4), 675–700.

Becker, Gary S., Michael Grossman, and Kevin M. Murphy (1994) An Empirical Analysis of Cigarette Addiction. *American Economic Review* 84(3), 396–418.

Becker, Gordon M., Morris H. DeGroot, and Jacob Marschak (1964) Measuring Utility by a Single-Response Sequential Method. *Behavioral Science* 9(3), 226–232.

Begley, Sharon and Toni Clarke (2015) Exclusive: US To Roll Back "Lost Pleasure" Approach on Health Rules. *Reuters*. March 18.

Benington, John and Mark H. Moore, eds. (2010) *Public Value: Theory and Practice*. New York: Palgrave Macmillan.

Bernheim, B. Douglas (2009) Behavioral Welfare Economics. *Journal of the European Economic Association* 7(2–3), 267–319.

(2016) The Good, the Bad, and the Ugly: A Unified Approach to Behavioral Welfare Economics. *Journal of Benefit-Cost Analysis* 7(1), 12–68.

Bernheim, B. Douglas and Antonio Rangel (2004) Addiction and Cue-Triggered Decision Processes. *American Economic Review* 94(5), 1558–1590.

(2007) Toward Choice-Theoretic Foundations for Behavioral Welfare Economics. *American Economic Review* 97(2), 464–470.

(2009) Beyond Revealed Preference: Choice-Theoretic Foundations for Behavioral Welfare Economics. *Quarterly Journal of Economics* 124(1), 51–104.

Bernheim, B. Douglas, Andrey Fradkin, and Igor Popov (2015) The Welfare Economics of Default Options in 401(k) Plans. *American Economic Review* 105(9), 2798–2837.

Berrens, Robert P., Alok K. Bohara, Hank C. Jenkins-Smith, Carol L. Silva, and David L. Weimer (2004) Information and Effort in Contingent Valuation Surveys: Application to Global Climate Change Using National Internet Samples. *Journal of Environmental Economics and Management* 47(2), 331–363.

Beshears, John, James J. Choi, David Laibson, and Brigitte C. Madrian (2008) How Are Preferences Revealed? *Journal of Public Economics* 92(8), 1787–1794.

(2009) The Importance of Default Options for Retirement Saving Outcomes: Evidence from the United States. In Jeffrey Brown, Jeffrey Liebman, and David A. Wise, editors, *Social Security Policy in a Changing Environment*. Chicago: University of Chicago Press, 167–195.

Bhargava, Saurabh and George Loewenstein (2015) Behavioral Economics and Public Policy 102: Beyond Nudging. *American Economic Review* 105(5), 396–401.

Bickel, Warren K., Matthew W. Johnson, Mikhail N. Koffarnus, James MacKillop, and James G. Murphy (2014) The Behavioral Economics of Substance Use Disorders: Reinforcement Pathologies and their Repair. *Annual Review of Clinical Psychology*, 641–677.

Bickel, Warren K. and Lisa A. Marsch (2001) Toward a Behavioral Economic Understanding of Drug Dependence: Delay Discounting Processes. *Addiction* 96(1), 73–86.

Bishop, Richard C. and Thomas A. Heberlein (1990) The Contingent Valuation Method. In Rebecca L. Johnson and Gary V. Johnson, Editors, *Economic Valuation of Natural Resources: Issues, Theory, and Applications*. Boulder: Westview Press, 81–104.

Blackorby, Charles and David Donaldson (1990) A Review Article: The Case against the Use of the Sum of Compensating Variations in Cost-benefit Analysis. *Canadian Journal of Economics* 23(3), 471–494.

Bleichrodt, Han, Jose Luis Pinto, and Peter P. Wakker (2001) Making Descriptive Use of Prospect Theory to Improve the Prescriptive Use of Expected Utility. *Management Science* 47(11), 1498–1514.

Blomquist, Glenn C. and John C. Whitehead (1998) Resource Quality Information and Validity of Willingness to Pay in Contingent Valuation. *Resource and Energy Economics* 20(2), 179–196.

Blumenschein, Karen, Glenn C. Blomquist, Magnus Johannesson, Nancy Horn, and Patricia Freeman (2008) Eliciting Willingness to Pay without Bias: Evidence from a Field Experiment. *Economic Journal* 118(525), 114–137.

Boadway, Robin W. (1974) The Welfare Foundation of Cost-Benefit Analysis. *Economic Journal* 84(336), 926–939.

Boadway, Robin W. and Neil Bruce (1984) *Welfare Economics*. New York: Basil Blackwell.

Boardman, Anthony E., David H. Greenberg, Aidan R. Vining, and David L. Weimer (2011) *Cost–Benefit Analysis: Concepts and Practice*, 4th ed. Upper Saddle River: Prentice Hall.

Boyer, Marcel (1983) Rational Demand and Expenditures Patterns under Habit Formation. *Journal of Economic Theory* 31(1), 27–53.

Bradford, David F. (1975) Constraints on Government Investment Opportunities and the Choice of Discount Rate. *The American Economic Review* 65(5), 887–899.

Brennan, Timothy J. (2014) Behavioral Economics and Policy Evaluation. *Journal of Benefit-Cost Analysis* 5(1), 89–109.

Brookshire, David S. and Don L. Coursey (1987) Measuring the Value of a Public Good: An Empirical Comparison of Elicitation Procedures. *American Economic Review* 77(4), 554–566.

Bromley, Daniel W. (1990) The Ideology of Efficiency: Searching for a Theory of Policy Analysis. *Journal of Environmental Economics and Management* 19(1), 86–107.

Bronsteen, John, Christopher J. Buccafusco, and Jonathan S. Masur (2013) Well-Being Analysis vs. Cost-Benefit Analysis. *Duke Law Journal* 62(8), 1603–1689.

Burgess, David F. and Richard O. Zerbe. (2011) Appropriate Discounting for Benefit-Cost Analysis. *Journal of Benefit-Cost Analysis* 2(2), 1–20.

(2013) The Most Appropriate Discount Rate. *Journal of Benefit-Cost Analysis* 4(3), 391–400.

Bushong, Benjamin, Lindsay M. King, Colin F. Camerer, and Antonio Rangel (2010) Pavlovian Processes in Consumer Choice: The Physical Presence of a Good Increases Willingness-to-Pay. *American Economic Review* 100(4), 1556–1571.

Cadena, Brian C. and Benjamin J. Keys (2015) Human Capital and the Lifetime Costs of Impatience. *American Economic Journal: Economic Policy* 7(3), 126–153.

Camerer, Colin, George Loewenstein, and Martin Weber (1989) The Curse of Knowledge in Economic Settings: An Experimental Analysis. *Journal of Political Economy* 97(5), 1232–1254.

Camerer, Colin F. (1987) Do Biases in Probability Judgment Matter in Markets? Experimental Evidence. *American Economic Review* 77(3), 981–997.

  (2004) Prospect Theory in the Wild: Evidence from the Field. In Colin F. Cramerer, George Loewenstein, and Matthew Rabin, Editors, *Advances in Behavioral Economics*. Princeton: Princeton University Press, 148–161.

Camerer, Colin F. and George Loewenstein (2004) Behavioral Economics: Past, Present, Future. In Colin F. Camerer, George Loewenstein, and Matthew Rabin, Editors, *Advances in Behavioral Economics*. Princeton: Princeton University Press, 3–51.

Camerer, Colin F. and Howard Kunreuther (1989) Decision Processes for Low Probability Events: Policy Implications. *Journal of Policy Analysis and Management* 8(4), 565–592.

Cameron, Trudy Ann (2010) Euthanizing the Value of a Statistical Life. *Review of Environmental Economics and Policy* 4(2), 161–178.

Campbell, Donald T. and Julian C. Stanley (1963) *Experimental and Quasi-Experimental Designs for Generalized Causal Inference*. Boston: Houghton Mifflin.

Campbell, John Y., Howell E. Jackson, Brigitte C. Madrian, and Peter Tufano (2011) Consumer Financial Protection. *Journal of Economic Perspectives* 25(1), 91–114.

Canada, Treasury Board (2007) *Canadian Cost-Benefit Analysis Guide: Regulatory Proposals*. Ottawa.

Carlson, Deven E., Joseph T. Ripberger, Hank C. Jenkins-Smith, Carol L. Silva, Kuhika Gupta, Robert P. Berrens, and Benjamin A. Jones (2016) Contingent Valuation and the Policymaking Process: An Application to Used Nuclear Fuel in the United States. *Journal of Benefit-Cost Analysis* 7(3), 459–487.

Carlsson, Fredrik, O. L. O. F. Johansson-Stenman, and Peter Martinsson (2007) Do You Enjoy Having More than Others? Survey Evidence of Positional Goods. *Economica* 74(296), 586–598.

Carson, Richard T. (2012) Contingent Valuation: A Practical Alternative when Prices Aren't Available. *Journal of Economic Perspectives* 26(4), 27–42.

Carson, Richard T., Nicholas E. Flores, and Norman F. Meade (2001) Contingent Valuation: Controversies and Evidence. *Environmental and Resource Economics* 19(2), 173–210.

Carson, Richard T. and Theodore Groves (2007) Incentive and Informational Properties of Preference Questions. *Environmental and Resource Economics* 37(1), 181–210.

Carter, Steven and Michael McBride (2013) Experienced Utility versus Decision Utility: Putting the "S" in Satisfaction. *The Journal of Socio-Economics* 42(1), 13–23.

Cartwright, Edward (2011) *Behavioral Economics*. London: Routledge.

Chabris, Christopher F., David I. Laibson, and Jonathon P. Schuldt (2008) Intertemporal Choice. In Steven N. Durlauf and Lawrence E. Blume, editors, *The New Palgrave Dictionary of Economics*, 2nd Edn. New York: Palgrave Macmillan, 1–12.

Chaloupka, Frank J., Jonathan Gruber, and Kenneth E. Warner (2015) Accounting for "Lost Pleasure" in Cost-Benefit Analysis of Government Regulation: The Case of Food and Drug Administration's Proposed Cigarette Labeling Regulation. *Annals of Internal Medicine* 161(1), 64–65.

Chambers, John R. and Paul D. Windschitl (2004) Biases in Social Comparative Judgments: The Role of Nonmotivated Factors in Above-Average and Comparative-Optimism Effects. *Psychological Bulletin* 130(5), 813–838.

Champ, Patricia A., Richard C. Bishop, Thomas C. Brown, and Daniel W. McCollum (1997) Using Donation Mechanisms to Value Nonuse Benefits from Public Goods. *Journal of Environmental Economics and Management* 33(2), 151–162.

Cherry, Todd L., Thomas D. Crocker, and Jason F. Shogren (2003) Rationality Spillovers. *Journal of Environmental Economics and Management* 45(1), 63–84.

Chetty, Raj (2015) Behavioral Economics and Public Policy: A Pragmatic Perspective. *American Economic Review* 105(5), 1–33.

Chetty, Raj, Adam Looney, and Kory Kroft (2009) Salience and Taxation: Theory and Evidence. *American Economic Review* 99(4), 1145–1177.

Chichilnisky, Graciela (1996) An Axiomatic Approach to Sustainable Development. *Social Choice and Welfare* 13(2), 231–257.

Cicchetti, Charles J. and A. Myrick Freeman III (1971) Option Demand and Consumer Surplus: Further Comment. *Quarterly Journal of Economics* 85(3), 528–539.

Clarke, Harry and Martin Byford (2009) Addictive Drug Use Management Policies in a Long-Run Economic Model. *Australian Economic Papers* 48(2), 151–165.

Compton, Wilson M. and Nora D. Volkow (2006) Abuse of Prescription Drugs and the Risk of Addiction. *Drug and Alcohol Dependence* 83(S1), S4–S7.

Copeland, Curtis W. (2011) *Cost-Benefit and Other Analysis Requirements in the Rulemaking Process*. Washington DC: Congressional Research Service.

Corso, Phaedra S., James K. Hammitt, and John D. Graham (2001) Valuing Mortality-Risk Reduction: Using Visual Aids to Improve the Validity of Contingent Valuation. *Journal of Risk and Uncertainty* 23(2), 165–184.

Courtney, Kelly E., Joseph P. Schacht, Kent Hutchison, Daniel JO Roche, and Lara A. Ray (2016) Neural Substrates of Cue Reactivity: Association with Treatment Outcomes and Relapse. *Addiction Biology* 21(1), 3–22.

Cox, James C. and David M. Grether (1996) The Preference Reversal Phenomenon: Response Mode, Markets and Incentives. *Economic Theory* 7(3), 381–405.

Cox, James C. and R. Isaac (1984) In Search of the Winner's Curse. *Economic Inquiry* 22(4), 579–592.

Cropper, Maureen, James K. Hammitt, and Lisa A. Robinson (2011) Valuing Mortality Risk Reductions: Progress and Challenges. *Annual Review of Resource Economics* 3, 313–336.

Cutler, David M., Amber Jessup, Donald Kenkel, and Martha A. Starr (2015) Valuing Regulations Affecting Addictive or Habitual Goods. *Journal of Benefit-Cost Analysis* 6(2), 247–280.

Dahlby, Bev (2008) *The Marginal Cost of Public Funds: Theory and Applications.* Cambridge, MA: MIT Press.

Daniel, Kent and David Hirshleifer (2015) Overconfident Investors, Predictable Returns, and Excessive Trading. *Journal of Economic Perspectives* 29(4), 61–88.

Deaton, Angus and John Muellbauer (1980) *Economics and Consumer Behavior.* New York: Cambridge University Press.

de Bekker-Grob, Esther W., Mandy Ryan, and Karen Gerard. (2012) Discrete Choice Experiments in Health Economics: A Review of the Literature. *Health Economics* 21(2), 145–172.

Deighton-Smith, Rex, Angelo Erbacci, and Céline Kauffmann (2016) *Promoting Inclusive Growth through Better Regulation: The Role of Regulatory Impact Assessment.* OECD Regulatory Policy Working Papers, No. 3 (Paris: OECD Publishing).

DellaVigna, Stefano and Ulrike Malmendier (2006) Paying Not to Go to the Gym. *The American Economic Review* 96(3), 694–719.

del Saz-Salazar, Salvador, Leandro García-Menéndez, and María Feo-Valero (2012) Meeting the Environmental Challenge of Port Growth: A Critical Appraisal of the Contingent Valuation Method and an Application to Valencia Port, Spain. *Ocean and Coastal Management* 59(April), 31–39.

DiFranza, Joseph R., Judith A. Savageau, Kenneth Fletcher, Jennifer O'Loughlin, Lori Pbert, Judith K. Ockene, Ann D. McNeill, Jennifer Hazelton, Karen Friedman, Gretchen Dussault, Connie Wood, and Robert J. Wellman (2007) Symptoms of Tobacco Dependence after Brief Intermittent Use: The Development and Assessment of Nicotine Dependence in Youth-2 Study. *Archives of Pediatrics and Adolescent Medicine* 161(7), 704–710.

Do, Amy M., Alexander V. Rupert, and George Wolford (2008) Evaluations of Pleasurable Experiences: The Peak-End Rule. *Psychonomic Bulletin & Review* 15(1), 96–98.

Ellsberg, Daniel (1961) Risk, Ambiguity, and the Savage Axioms. *Quarterly Journal of Economics* 75(4), 643–669.

Ericson, Keith M., John Myles White, David Laibson, and Jonathan D. Cohen (2015) Money Earlier or Later? Simple Heuristics Explain Intertemporal Choices Better than Delay Discounting Does. *Psychological Science* 26(6), 826–833.

Evans, Dorla A. (1997) The Role of Markets in Reducing Expected Utility Violations. *Journal of Political Economy* 105(3), 622–636.

Flores, Nicholas E. and Richard T. Carson (1997) The Relationship between the Income Elasticities of Demand and Willingness to Pay. *Journal of Environmental Economics and Management* 33(3), 287–295.

Florio, Massimo (2006) Cost-Benefit Analysis and the European Union Cohesion Fund: On the Social Cost of Capital and Labour. *Regional Studies* 40(2), 211–224.

Fon, Vincy and Yoshihiko Otani (1979) Classical Welfare Theorems with Non-Transitive and Non-Complete Preferences. *Journal of Economic Theory* 20(3), 409–418.

Fox, Chris and Kevin Albertson (2011) Payment by Results and Social Impact Bonds in the Criminal Justice Sector: New Challenges for the Concept of Evidence-Based Policy? *Criminology and Criminal Justice* 11(5), 395–413.

Frederick, Shane, George Loewenstein, and Ted O'Donoghue (2002) Time Discounting and Time Preference: A Critical Review. *Journal of Economic Literature* 40(2), 351–401.

Freeman III, A. Myrick, Joseph A. Herriges, and Catherine L. Kling (2014) *The Measurement of Environmental and Resource Values: Theory and Methods.* New York: Routledge

Fudenberg, Drew and David K. Levina (2011) Risk, Delay, and Convex Self-Control Costs. *American Economic Journal: Microeconomics* 3(3), 34–68.

Gately, Dermot (1980) Individual Discount Rates and the Purchase and Utilization of Energy-Using Durables: Comment. *Bell Journal of Economics* 11(1), 373–374.

Gayer, Ted and W. Kip Viscusi (2013) Overriding Consumer Preferences with Energy Regulations. *Journal of Regulatory Economics* 43(3), 248–264.

Gollier, Christian and James K. Hammitt (2014) The Long-Run Discount Rate Controversy. *Annual Review of Resource Economics* 6(1), 273–295.

Goodman, Aviel (2008) Neurobiology of Addiction: An Integrative Review. *Biochemical Pharmacology* 75(1), 266–322.

Goodman, Madeline, Robert Finnegan, Leyla Mohadjer, Tom Krenzke, and Jacquie Hogan (2013) *Literacy, Numeracy, and Problem Solving in Technology-Rich Environments Among US Adults: Results from the Program for the International Assessment of Adult Competencies 2012: First Look.* Washington, DC: US Department of Education, National Center for Education Statistics.

Gowdy, John M. (2004) The Revolution in Welfare Economics and Its Implications for Environmental Valuation and Policy. *Land Economics* 80(2), 239–257.

Graham, Daniel A. (1981) Cost-Benefit Analysis under Uncertainty. *American Economic Review* 71(4), 715–725.

Groves, Theodore and John Ledyard (1977) Optimal Allocation of Public Goods: A Solution to the "Free Rider" Problem. *Econometrica* 45(4), 783–809.

Grubb, Michael D. (2015) Overconfident Consumers in the Marketplace. *Journal of Economic Perspectives* 29(4), 9–36.

Gruber, Jonathan and Botond Köszegi (2001) Is Addiction "Rational"? Theory and Evidence. *Quarterly Journal of Economics* 116(4), 1261–1303.

Gul, Faruk and Wolfgang Pesendorfer (2004) Self-Control, Revealed Preference and Consumption Choice. *Review of Economic Dynamics* 7(2), 243–264.

(2005) The Revealed Preference Theory of Changing Tastes. *Review of Economic Studies* 72(2), 429–448.

(2007) Harmful Addiction. *Review of Economic Studies* 74(1), 147–172.

Haab, Timothy C. and Kenneth E. McConnell (2003) *Valuing Environmental and Natural Resources: The Econometrics of Non-Market Valuation.* Northampton: Edward Elgar Publishing.

Hahn, Robert W. and Paul C. Tetlock (2008) Has Economic Analysis Improved Regulatory Decisions? *Journal of Economic Perspectives* 22(1), 67–84.

Hall, Wayne, Adrian Carter, and Cynthia Forlini (2015) The Brain Disease Model of Addiction: Is It Supported by the Evidence and Has It Delivered on Its Promises? *Lancet Psychiatry* 2(1), 105–110.

Hammitt, James K. (2015) Implications of the WTP–WTA Disparity for Benefit–Cost Analysis. *Journal of Benefit-Cost Analysis* 6(1), 207–216.

Hammitt, James K. and John D. Graham (1999) Willingness to Pay for Health Protection: Inadequate Sensitivity to Probability? *Journal of Risk and Uncertainty* 18(1), 33–62.

Hammond, Peter J. (1981) Ex-Ante and Ex-Post Welfare Optimality under Uncertainty. *Economica* 48(191), 235–250.

Hammond, Richard J. (1966) Convention and Limitation in Benefit-Cost Analysis. *Natural Resources Journal* 6(2), 195–222.

Hanemann, W. Michael (1991) Willingness to Pay and Willingness to Accept: How Much Can They Differ? *American Economic Review* 81(3), 635–647.

Hanley, Nick and Jason F. Shogren (2005) Is Cost–Benefit Analysis Anomaly-Proof? *Environmental and Resource Economics* 32(1), 13–24.

Hanley, Nick and Clive L. Spash (1993) *Cost-Benefit Analysis and the Environment.* Northampton: Edward Elgar.

Harris, Richard and Nancy Olewiler (1979) The Welfare Economics of Ex Post Optimality. *Economica* 46(182), 137–147.

Harrison, Glenn W. and E. Elisabet Rutström (2009) Expected Utility Theory and Prospect Theory: One Wedding and a Decent Funeral. *Experimental Economics* 12(2), 133–158.

Harrison, Mark, Dan Rigby, Caroline Vass, Terry Flynn, Jordan Louviere, and Katherine Payne (2014) Risk as an Attribute in Discrete Choice Experiments: A Systematic Review of the Literature. *Patient* 7(2), 151–170.

Hausman, Jerry A. (1979) Individual Discount Rates and the Purchase and Utilization of Energy-Using Durables. *Bell Journal of Economics* 10(1), 33–54.

(2012) Contingent Valuation: From Dubious to Hopeless. *Journal of Economic Perspectives* 26(4), 43–56.

Haveman, Robert H. and David L. Weimer (2015) Public Policy Induced Changes in Employment: Valuation Issues for Benefit-Cost Analysis. *Journal of Benefit-Cost Analysis* 6(1), 112–153.

Hawkins, James, William Hollingworth, and Rona Campbell (2010) Long-Term Smoking Relapse: A Study Using the British Household Panel Survey. *Nicotine and Tobacco Research* 12(12), 1228–1235.

Heberlein, Thomas A., Matthew A. Wilson, Richard C. Bishop, and Nora Cate Schaeffer (2005) Rethinking the Scope Test as a Criterion for Validity in Contingent Valuation. *Journal of Environmental Economics and Management* 50(1), 1–22.

Herrnstein, Richard J., George F. Loewenstein, Drazen Prelec, and William Vaughan (1993) Utility Maximization and Melioration: Internalities in Individual Choice. *Journal of Behavioral Decision Making* 6(3), 149–185.

Hershey, John C. and Paul J. H. Schoemaker (1985) Probability Versus Certainty Equivalence Methods in Utility Measurement: Are They Equivalent? *Management Science* 31(10), 1213–1231.

Hicks, John R. (1939) The Foundations of Welfare Economics. *Economic Journal* 49(196), 696–712.

(1940) The Valuation of the Social Income. *Economica* 7(26), 105–124.

(1941) The Rehabilitation of Consumers' Surplus. *Review of Economic Studies* 8(2), 108–116.

(1942) Consumers' Surplus and Index-Numbers. *Review of Economic Studies* 9 (2), 126–137.

Hersch, Joni (2005) Smoking Restrictions as a Self-Control Mechanism. *Journal of Risk and Uncertainty* 31(1), 5–21.

Horowitz, John K. and Kenneth E. McConnell (2002) A Review of WTA/WTP Studies. *Journal of Environmental Economics and Management* 44(3), 426–447.

Horwich, George, Hank Jenkins-Smith, and David L. Weimer (1988) The International Energy Agency's Mandatory Oil-Sharing Agreement: Tests of Efficiency, Equity, and Practicality. In George Horwich and David L. Weimer, eds., *Responding to International Oil Crises* (Washington, DC: American Enterprise Institute for Public Policy), 104–133.

Hotelling, Harold (1938) The General Welfare in Relation to Problems of Taxation and of Railway and Utility Rates. *Econometrica* 6(3), 242–269.

Iannaccone, Laurence R. (1986) Addiction and Satiation. *Economics Letters* 21(1), 95–99.

Ida, Takanori (2014) A Quasi-Hyperbolic Discounting Approach to Smoking Behavior. *Health Economics Review* 4(1), 1–11.

Independent Evaluation Group (2010) Cost-Benefit Analysis in World Bank Projects. World Bank Fast Track Brief 57037. June 4.

Jacquemet, Nicolas, Robert-Vincent Joule, Stéphane Luchini, and Jason F. Shogren (2013) Preference Elicitation under Oath. *Journal of Environmental Economics and Management* 65(1), 110–132.

Jin, Lawrence, Don Kenkel, Feng Liu, and Hua Wang (2015). Retrospective and Prospective Benefit-Cost Analyses of US Anti-Smoking Policies. *Journal of Benefit-Cost Analysis* 6(1), 154–186.

Johnson, Sara B., Robert W. Blum, and Jay N. Giedd (2009) Adolescent Maturity and the Brain: The Promise and Pitfalls of Neuroscience Research in Adolescent Health Policy. *Journal of Adolescent Health* 45(3), 216–221.

Jones-Lee, M. W., M. Hammerton, and P. R. Philips (1985) The Value of Safety: Results of a National Sample Survey. *Economic Journal* 95(377), 49–72.

Just, Richard W., Darrell L. Hueth, and Andrew Schmitz (2004) *The Welfare Economics of Public Policy: A Practical Approach to Project and Policy Evaluation*. Northampton: Edward Elgar.

Kahan, Dan M. (2013) Ideology, Motivated Reasoning, and Cognitive Reflection: An Experimental Study. *Judgment and Decision Making* 8(4), 407–424.

Kahan, Dan M., Hank Jenkins-Smith, Tor Tarantola, Carol L. Silva, and Donald Braman (2015) Geoengineering and Climate Change Polarization Testing a Two-Channel Model of Science Communication. *ANNALS of the American Academy of Political and Social Science* 658(1), 192–222.

Kahneman, Daniel (1994) New Challenges to the Rationality Assumption. *Journal of Institutional and Theoretical Economics* 150(1), 18–36.

Kahneman, Daniel, Jack L. Knetsch, and Richard H. Thaler (1990) Experimental Tests of the Endowment Effect and the Coase Theorem. *Journal of Political Economy* 98(6), 1325–1348.

Kahneman, Daniel and Robert Sugden (2005) Experienced Utility as a Standard of Policy Evaluation. *Environmental and Resource Economics* 32(1), 161–181.

Kahneman, Daniel and Richard H. Thaler (1991) Economic Analysis and the Psychology of Utility: Applications to Compensation Policy. *American Economic Review* 81(2), 341–346.

(2006) Anomalies: Utility Maximization and Experienced Utility. *Journal of Economic Perspectives* 20(1), 221–234

Kahneman, Daniel and Amos Tversky (1979) Prospect Theory: An Analysis of Decision under Risk. *Econometrica* 47(2), 263–291.

(1984) Choices, Values, and Frames. *American Psychologist* 39(4), 341–350.

Kahneman, Daniel, Peter P. Wakker, and Rakesh Sarin (1997) Back to Bentham? Explorations of Experienced Utility. *Quarterly Journal of Economics*, 112(2), 375–405.

Kaldor, Nicholas (1939) Welfare Propositions of Economics and Interpersonal Comparisons of Utility. *Economic Journal* 49(195), 549–552.

Kanbur, Ravi, Jukka Pirttilä, and Matti Tuomala (2008) Moral Hazard, Income Taxation and Prospect Theory. *The Scandinavian Journal of Economics* 110(2), 321–337.

Karsenty, Alain, Aurélie Vogel, and Frédéric Castell (2014) "Carbon Rights," REDD+ and Payments for Environmental Services. *Environmental Science & Policy* 35(January), 20–29.

Klaiber, H. Allen and V. Kerry Smith (2012) Developing General Equilibrium Benefit Analyses for Social Programs: An Introduction and Example. *Journal of Benefit-Cost Analysis* 3(2), 1–52.

Knetsch, Jack L. (1990) Environmental Policy Implications of Disparities between Willingness to Pay and Compensation Demanded Measures of Values. *Journal of Environmental Economics and Management* 18(3), 227–237.

(2015) The Curiously Continuing Saga of Choosing the Measure of Welfare Changes. *Journal of Benefit-Cost Analysis* 6(1), 217–225.

Knetsch, Jack L., Yohanes E. Riyanto, and Jichuan Zong (2012) Gain and Loss Domains and the Choice of Welfare Measure of Positive and Negative Changes. *Journal of Benefit-Cost Analysis* 3(4), 1–18.

Kőszegi, Botond and Matthew Rabin (2008) Choices, Situations, and Happiness. *Journal of Public Economics* 92(8), 1821–1832.

Kniesner, Thomas J., W. Kip Viscusi, and James P. Ziliak (2014). Willingness to Accept Equals Willingness to Pay for Labor Market Estimates of the Value of a Statistical Life. *Journal of Risk and Uncertainty* 48(3), 187–205.

Kozel, Nicholas J. and Edgar H. Adams (1986) Epidemiology of Drug Abuse: An Overview. *Science* 234(4779), 970–974.

Krishna, Vijesh V., Adam G. Drucker, Unai Pascual, Prabhakaran T. Raghu, and E.D. Israel Oliver King (2013) Estimating Compensation Payments for On-Farm Conservation of Agricultural Biodiversity in Developing Countries. *Ecological Economics* 87(March), 110–123.

Laibson, David (1997) Golden Eggs and Hyperbolic Discounting. *Quarterly Journal of Economics* 112(2), 443–477.

(2001) A Cue-Theory of Consumption. *Quarterly Journal of Economics* 116 (1), 81–119.

Larrick, Richard P. and Jack B. Soll (2008) The MPG Illusion. *Science* 320(5883), 1593–1594.

Larson, Douglas M. and Paul R. Flacco (1992) Measuring Option Prices from Market Behavior. *Journal of Environmental Economics and Management* 22 (2), 178–198.

Laux, Fritz L. (2000) Addiction as a Market Failure: Using Rational Addiction Results to Justify Tobacco Regulation. *Journal of Health Economics* 19(4), 421–437.

Le Grand, Julian and Bill New (2015) *Government Paternalism: Nanny State or Helpful Friend?* Princeton: Princeton University Press.

Leshner, Alan I. (1997) Addiction Is a Brain Disease, and It Matters. *Science* 278(5335), 45–47.

Levy, Neil (2013) Addiction Is Not a Brain Disease (and It Matters). *Frontiers in Psychiatry* 4(24.10), 3389–3395.

Levy, Daniel S. and David Friedman (1994) The Revenge of the Redwoods? Reconsidering Property Rights and the Economic Allocation of Natural Resources. *University of Chicago Law Review* 61(2), 493–526.

Lewis, Marc (2015) *The Biology of Desire: Why Addiction Is Not a Disease.* New York: PublicAffairs,

Li, Chuan-Zhong, and Leif Mattsson (1995) Discrete Choice under Preference Uncertainty: An Improved Structural Model for Contingent Valuation. *Journal of Environmental Economics and Management* 28(2), 256–269.

Li, Hui, Robert P. Berrens, Alok K. Bohara, Hank C. Jenkins-Smith, Carol L. Silva, and David L. Weimer (2005) Testing for Budget Constraint Effects in a National Advisory Referendum Survey on the Kyoto Protocol. *Journal of Agricultural and Resource Economics* 30(2), 350–366.

Lichtenstein, Sarah and Paul Slovic, Editors (1971) Reversals of Preferences between Bids and Choices in Gambling Decisions. *Journal of Experimental Psychology* 89(1), 46–55.

(2006) *The Construction of Preferences.* New York: Cambridge University Press.

Lichtenstein, Sarah, Paul Slovic, Baruch Fischhoff, Mark Layman, and Barbara Combs (1978) Judged Frequency of Lethal Events. *Journal of Experimental Psychology* 4(6), 551–578.

Lindhjem, Henrik, Ståle Navrud, Nils Axel Braathen, and Vincent Biausque (2011) Valuing Mortality Risk Reductions from Environmental, Transport,

References

and Health Policies: A Global Meta-Analysis of Stated Preference Studies. *Risk Analysis* 31(9), 1381–1407.

Loewenstein, George and Jennifer S. Lerner (2003) The Role of Affect in Decision Making. *Handbook of Affective Science* 3, 619–642.

Loewenstein, George, Ted O'Donoghue, and Mathew Rabin (2003) Projection Bias in Predicting Future Utility. *Quarterly Journal of Economics* 118(4), 1209–1248.

Loewenstein, George and Drazen Prelec (1992) Anomalies in Intertemporal Choice: Evidence and an Interpretation. *Quarterly Journal of Economics* 107(2), 573–597.

Loewenstein, George and Peter A. Ubel (2008) Hedonic Adaptation and the Role of Decision and Experience Utility in Public Policy. *Journal of Public Economics* 92(8), 1795–1810.

Long, David A., Charles D. Mallar, and Craig V.D. Thornton (1981) Evaluating the Benefits and Costs of the Job Corps. *Journal of Policy Analysis and Management* 1(1), 55–76.

Loomis, John B. (2014) Strategies for Overcoming Hypothetical Bias in Stated Preference Surveys. *Journal of Agricultural and Resource Economics* 39(1), 34–46.

Loomis, John B. and Pierre H. duVair (1993) Evaluating the Effect of Alternative Risk Communication Devices on Willingness to Pay: Results from a Dichotomous Choice Contingent Valuation Experiment. *Land Economics* 69(3), 287–298.

Luhmann, Christian C. (2013) Discounting of Delayed Rewards Is Not Hyperbolic. *Journal of Experimental Psychology: Learning, Memory, and Cognition* 39(4), 1274–1279.

Lusardi, Annamaria and Olivia S. Mitchell (2007) Baby Boomer Retirement Security: The Roles of Planning, Financial Literacy, and Housing Wealth. *Journal of Monetary Economics* 54(1), 205–224.

Lutter, Randall (2013) Regulatory Policy: What Role for Retrospective Analysis and Review? *Journal of Benefit-Cost Analysis* 4(1), 17–38.

Lyon, Randolph M. (1990) Federal Discount Rate Policy, the Shadow Price of Capital, and Challenges for Reforms. *Journal of Environmental Economics and Management* 18(2), S29–S50.

Machina, Mark J. (1982) "Expected Utility" Analysis without the Independence Axiom. *Econometrica* 50(2), 277–323.

Madrian, Brigitte C. (2014) Applying Insights from Behavioral Economics to Policy Design. *Annual Review of Economics* 6, 663–688.

Madrian, Brigitte C. and Dennis F. Shea (2001) The Power of Suggestion: Inertia in 401(k) Participation and Savings Behavior. *Quarterly Journal of Economics* 116(4), 1149–1187.

Malmendier, Ulrike and Timothy Taylor (2015) On the Verges of Overconfidence. *Journal of Economic Perspectives* 29(4), 3–8.

Mäntymaa, Erkki (1999) Pennies from Heaven? A Test of the Social Budget Constraint in a Willingness to Accept Compensation Elicitation Format. *Journal of Forest Economics* 5(1), 169–192.

McFadden, Daniel (1974) Conditional Logit Analysis of Qualitative Choice Behavior. In Paul Zarembka, ed. *Frontiers in Econometrics*. New York: Academic Press, 105–142.

McClelland, Gary H., William D. Schulze, and Don L. Coursey (1993) Insurance for Low-Probability Hazards: A Bimodal Response to Unlikely Events. *Journal of Risk and Uncertainty* 7(1), 95–116.

Melberg, Hans O. and Ole J. Rogeberg (2010) Rational Addiction Theory: A Survey of Opinions. *Journal of Drug Policy Analysis* 3(1), 1–9.

Millar, Ross and Kelly Hall (2013) Social Return on Investment (SROI) and Performance Measurement. *Public Management Review* 15(6), 923–941.

Miller, George A. (1956) The Magical Number Seven, Plus or Minus Two: Some Limits on Our Capacity for Processing Information. *Psychological Review* 63(2), 81–96.

Mishan, Ezra J. (1976) The Use of Compensating and Equivalent Variation in Cost-Benefit Analysis. *Economica* 43(170), 185–197.

Monterosso, John, Payam Piray, and Shan Luo (2012) Neuroeconomics and the Study of Addiction. *Biological Psychiatry* 72(2), 107–112.

Moore, Mark A., Anthony E. Boardman, and Aidan R. Vining. (2013a) More Appropriate Discounting: The Rate of Social Time Preference and the Value of the Social Discount Rate. *Journal of Benefit-Cost Analysis* 4(1), 1–16.

  (2013b) The Choice of the Social Discount Rate and the Opportunity Cost of Public Funds. *Journal of Benefit-Cost Analysis* 4(3), 401–409.

Moore, Mark A., Anthony E. Boardman, Aidan R. Vining, David L. Weimer, and David H. Greenberg (2004) "Just Give Me a Number!": Practical Values for the Social Discount Rate. *Journal of Policy Analysis and Management* 23(4), 789–812.

Moore, Mark H. (1995) *Creating Public Value: Strategic Management in Government*. Cambridge: Harvard University Press.

Moore, Michael J. and W. Kip Viscusi (1988) Doubling the Estimated Value of Life: Results Using New Occupational Fatality Data. *Journal of Policy Analysis and Management* 7(3), 476–490.

Morewedge, Carey K., Daniel T. Gilbert, Kristian Ove R. Myrseth, Karim S. Kassam, and Timothy D. Wilson (2010) Consuming Experience: Why Affective Forecasters Overestimate Comparative Value. *Journal of Experimental Social Psychology* 46(6), 986–992.

Morrison, Edward R. (1998) Judicial Review of Discount Rates Used in Regulatory Cost-Benefit Analyses. *University of Chicago Law Review* 65(4), 1333–1369.

Nechyba, Thomas J. (2000) Mobility, Targeting, and Private-School Vouchers. *American Economic Review* 90(1), 130–146.

Newell, Richard G. and Juha Siikamaki (2015) Individual Time Preferences and Energy Efficiency. *American Economic Review* 105(5), 196–200.

Niskanen, William A., Jr. (1991) A Reflection on *Bureaucracy and Representative Government*. In André Blaise and Stéphane Dion, Editors, *The Budget Maximizing Bureaucrat: Appraisals and Evidence*. Pittsburgh: University of Pittsburgh Press, 13–31.

Noonan, Douglas S. (2003) Contingent Valuation and Cultural Resources: A Meta-Analytic Review of the Literature. *Journal of Cultural Economics* 27(3–4), 159–176.

O'Donoghue, Ted and Matthew Rabin (1999) Doing It Now or Later. *American Economic Review* 89(1), 103–124.

(2015) Present Bias: Lessons Learned and to be Learned. *American Economic Review* 105(5), 273–279.

Oliver, Adam, ed. (2013) *Behavioral Public Policy*. New York: Cambridge University Press.

Olson, Mancur (1965) *Logic of Collective Action: Public Goods and the Theory of Groups*. Cambridge: Harvard University Press.

Persky, Joseph (2001) Retrospectives: Cost-Benefit Analysis and the Classical Creed. *Journal of Economic Perspectives* 15(4), 199–208.

Pew-MacArthur (2015) Results First Fact Sheet (www.pewtrusts.org/en/projects/pew-macarthur-results-first-initiative).

Phelps, Edmund S. and Robert A. Pollak (1968) On Second-Best National Saving and Game-Equilibrium Growth. *Review of Economic Studies* 35(2), 185–199.

Plott, Charles R. and Kathryn Zeiler (2005) The Willingness to Pay–Willingness to Accept Gap, the "Endowment Effect," Subject Misconceptions, and Experimental Procedures for Eliciting Valuations. *American Economic Review* 95(3), 530–545.

Quiggin, John (1982) A Theory of Anticipated Utility. *Journal of Economic Behavior and Organization* 3(4), 323–343.

Randall, Alan and John R. Stoll (1980) Consumer's Surplus in Commodity Space. *American Economic Review* 70(3), 449–455.

Ramsey, Frank P. (1928) A Mathematical Theory of Saving. *Economic Journal* 38 (152), 543–559.

Rasmusen, Eric (2012) Internalities and Paternalism: Applying the Compensation Criterion to Multiple Selves across Time. *Social Choice and Welfare* 38(4), 601–615.

Read, Daniel and George Loewenstein (1995) Diversification Bias: Explaining the Discrepancy in Variety Seeking between Combined and Separated Choices. *Journal of Experimental Psychology: Applied* 1(1), 34–49.

Redish, A. David, Steve Jensen, and Adam Johnson (2008) A Unified Framework for Addiction: Vulnerabilities in the Decision Process. *Behavioral and Brain Sciences* 31(4), 415–437.

Reyna, Valerie F. (2004) How People Make Decisions That Involve Risk: A Dual-Process Approach. *Current Directions in Psychological Science* 13(2), 60–66.

Richards, Timothy J. and Stephen F. Hamilton (2012) Obesity and Hyperbolic Discounting: An Experimental Analysis. *Journal of Agricultural and Resource Economics* 37(2), 181–198.

Richter, Linda and Susan E. Foster (2014) Effectively Addressing Addiction Requires Changing the Language of Addiction. *Journal of Public Health Policy* 35(1), 60–64.

Robinson, Lisa A. and James K. Hammitt (2011) Behavioral Economics and the Conduct of Benefit-Cost Analysis: Towards Principles and Standards. *Journal of Benefit-Cost Analysis* 2(2), 1–51.

(2013) Skills of the Trade: Valuing Health Risk Reductions in Benefit-Cost Analysis. *Journal of Benefit-Cost Analysis* 4(1), 107–130.

(2016) Valuing Reductions in Fatal Illness Risks: Implications of Recent Research. *Health Economics* 25(8), 1039–1052.

Robinson, Lisa, James K. Hammitt, and Richard Zeckhauser (2016) Attention to Distribution in US Regulatory Analysis. *Review of Environmental Economics and Policy* 10(2), 308–328.

Robson, Arthur J. and Balazs Szentes (2014) A Biological Theory of Social Discounting. *American Economic Review* 104(11), 3481–3497.

Rubinstein, Ariel (2003) "Economics and Psychology"? The Case of Hyperbolic Discounting. *International Economic Review* 44(4), 1207–1216.

Ryder, Harl E. and Geoffrey M. Heal (1973) Optimal Growth with Intertemporally Dependent Preferences. *Review of Economic Studies* 40(1), 1–31.

Samuelson, Paul A. (1937) A Note on Measurement of Utility. *Review of Economic Studies* 4(2), 155–161.

Sandmo, Agnar (1983) Ex Post Welfare Economics and the Theory of Merit Goods. *Economica* 50(197), 19–33.

Sayman, Serdar and Ayşe Öncüler (2005) Effects of Study Design Characteristics on the WTA–WTP Disparity: A Meta Analytical Framework. *Journal of Economic Psychology* 26(2), 289–312.

Scitovsky, Tibor (1941) A Note on Welfare Propositions in Economics. *Review of Economic Studies* 9(1), 77–88.

Sen, Amartya (1990) Rational Behaviour. In John Eatwell, Murray Milgate, and Peter Newman, Editors, *The New Palgrave: Utility and Probability*, 198–216.

Scharff, Robert L. and W. Kip Viscusi (2011) Heterogeneous Rates of Time Preference and the Decision to Smoke. *Economic Inquiry* 49(4), 959–972.

Schelling, Thomas C. (1984) Self-Command in Practice, in Policy, and in a Theory of Rational Choice. *American Economic Review* 74(2), 1–11.

Schkade, David A. and Daniel Kahneman (1998) Does Living in California Make People Happy? A Focusing Illusion in Judgments of Life Satisfaction. *Psychological Science* 9(5), 340–346.

Schmalensee, Richard (1972) Option Demand and Consumer's Surplus: Valuing Price Changes under Uncertainty. *American Economic Review* 62(5), 813–824.

Schmeidler, David (1989) Subjective Probability and Expected Utility without Additivity. *Econometrica* 57(3), 571–587.

Schmidt, Ulrich, Chris Starmer and Robert Sugden (2008) Third-Generation Prospect Theory. *Journal of Risk and Uncertainty* 36(3), 203–223.

Shapiro, Stuart and John F. Morrall III (2012) The Triumph of Regulatory Politics: Benefit–Cost Analysis and Political Salience. *Regulation & Governance* 6(2), 189–206.

Shogren, Jason F. and Linda Thunström (2016) Do We Need a New Behavioral Benchmark for BCA? *Journal of Benefit-Cost Analysis* 7(1), 92–106.

Sims, Sally and Peter Dent (2005) High-Voltage Overhead Power Lines and Property Values: A Residential Study in the UK. *Urban Studies* 42(4), 665–694.

Sloan, Frank A., Vincent Kerry Smith, and Donald H. Taylor (2003) *The Smoking Puzzle: Information, Risk Perception, and Choice*. Cambridge: Harvard University Press.

Sloan, Frank A., W. Kip Viscusi, Harrell W. Chesson, Christopher J. Conover, and Kathryn Whetten-Goldstein (1998) Alternative Approaches to Valuing Intangible Health Losses: The Evidence for Multiple Sclerosis. *Journal of Health Economics* 17(4), 475–497.

Slovic, Paul (1987) Perception of Risk. *Science* 236(4799), 280–285.

Smith, David E. (2012) The Process Addictions and the New ASAM Definition of Addiction. *Journal of Psychoactive Drugs* 44(1), 1–4.

Smith, Vernon L. (1980) Experiments with a Decentralized Mechanism for Public Good Decisions. *American Economic Review* 70(4), 584–599.

(1985) Experimental Economics: Reply. *American Economic Review* 75(1), 265–272.

Smith, V. Kerry and William H. Desvousges (1987) An Empirical Analysis of the Economic Value of Risk Changes. *Journal of Political Economy* 95(1), 89–114.

Smith, V. Kerry and Eric M. Moore (2010). Behavioral Economics and Benefit Cost Analysis. *Environmental and Resource Economics* 46(2), 217–234.

Smith, V. Kerry, Donald H. Taylor, and Frank A. Sloan (2001) Longevity Expectations and Death: Can People Predict their Own Demise? *American Economic Review* 91(4), 1126–1134.

Song, Anna V., Paul Brown, and Stanton A. Glantz (2014) When Health Policy and Empirical Evidence Collide: The Case of Cigarette Package Warning Labels and Economic Consumer Surplus. *American Journal of Public Health* 104(2), e42–e51.

Starmer, Chris (2000) Developments in Non-Expected Utility Theory: The Hunt for a Descriptive Theory of Choice under Risk. *Journal of Economic Literature* 38(2), 332–382.

Stigler, George J. and Gary S. Becker (1977) De Gustibus Non Est Disputandum. *American Economic Review* 67(2), 76–90.

Strotz, R. H. (1955–56) Myopia and Inconsistency in Dynamic Utility Maximization. *Review of Economic Studies* 23(3), 165–180.

Sturman, David A. and Bita Moghaddam (2011) The Neurobiology of Adolescence: Changes in Brain Architecture, Functional Dynamics, and Behavioral Tendencies. *Neuroscience & Biobehavioral Reviews* 35(8), 1704–1712.

Sugden, Robert (2004) The Opportunity Criterion: Consumer Sovereignty without the Assumption of Coherent Preferences. *American Economic Review* 94(4), 1014–1033.

(2005) Coping with Preference Anomalies in Cost–Benefit Analysis: A Market-Simulation Approach. *Environmental and Resource Economics* 32(1), 129–160.

(2008) Why Incoherent Preferences Do Dot Justify Paternalism. *Constitutional Political Economy* 19(3), 226–248.

(2009) On Nudging: A Review of *Nudge: Improving Decisions About Health, Wealth and Happiness* by Richard H. Thaler and Cass R. Sunstein. *International Journal of the Economics of Business* 16(3), 365–373.

Thaler, Richard H. (1981) Some Empirical Evidence on Dynamic Inconsistency. *Economics Letters* 8(3), 201–207.

(1988) Anomalies: The Winner's Curse. *Journal of Economic Perspectives* 2(1), 191–202.

Thaler, Richard H. and Shlomo Benartzi (2004) Save More Tomorrow™: Using Behavioral Economics to Increase Employee Saving. *Journal of Political Economy* 112(S1), S164–S187.

Thaler, Richard H. and Cass R. Sunstein (2003) Libertarian Paternalism. *American Economic Review* 93(2), 175–179.

(2008) *Nudge: Improving Decisions about Health, Wealth, and Happiness.* New Haven: Yale University Press.

Thompson, Fred and Polly Rizova (2015) Understanding and Creating Public Value: Business Is the Engine, Government the Flywheel (and also the Regulator). *Public Management Review* 17(4), 565–586.

Trumbull, William N. (1990) Who Has Standing in Cost-Benefit Analysis? *Journal of Policy Analysis and Management* 9(2), 201–218.

Tunçel, Tuba and James K. Hammitt (2014) A New Meta-Analysis on the WTP/ WTA Disparity. *Journal of Environmental Economics and Management* 68(1), 175–187.

Tversky, Amos and Daniel Kahneman (1974) Judgment under Uncertainty: Heuristics and Biases. *Science* 185(4157), 1124–1131.

(1992) Advances in Prospect Theory: Cumulative Representation of Uncertainty. *Journal of Risk and Uncertainty* 5(4), 297–323.

Ubel, Peter A., George Loewenstein, and Christopher Jepson (2003) Whose Quality of Life? A Commentary Exploring Discrepancies between Health State Evaluations of Patients and the General Public. *Quality of Life Research* 12(6), 599–607.

United Kingdom, HM Treasury (2003) *The Green Book: Appraisal and Evaluation in Central Government.* London: The Stationery Office.

United States, Centers for Disease Control and Prevention (2016) Smoking and Tobacco Use: Fact Sheet. www.cdc.gov/tobacco/data_statistics/fact_sheets/yo uth_data/tobacco_use/index.htm.

United States, Department of Health and Human Services (2014) *The Health Consequences of Smoking—50 Years of Progress: A Report of the Surgeon General.* Atlanta: US Department of Health and Human Services, Centers for Disease Control and Prevention, National Center for Chronic Disease Prevention and Health Promotion, Office on Smoking and Health.

United States, Department of Transportation (2014a) *Revised Departmental Guidance on the Valuation of Travel Time in Economic Analysis.* Office of Economic and Strategic Analysis. July 9.

(2014b) *Guidance on Treatment of the Economic Value of a Statistical Life (VSL) in US Department of Transportation Analyses—2014 Adjustment.* Acting Undersecretary for Policy and General Council. June 13.

United States, Environmental Protection Agency (2003) *Benefits and Costs of the Clean Air Act 1990–2020: Revised Analytical Plan For EPA's Second Prospective Analysis.* Office of Policy Analysis and Review. May 12.

(2010) *Valuing Mortality Risk Reductions for Environmental Policy: A White Paper.* National Center for Environmental Economics. Review Draft. December 10.

(2014) *Guidelines for Preparing Economic Analyses.* National Center for Environmental Economics.

(2015) *Economy-Wide Modeling: Benefits of Air Quality Improvements White Paper.* Prepared for the Science Advisory Board Panel on Economy-Wide Modeling of the Benefits and Costs of Environmental Regulation. September 22.

United States, Food and Drug Administration (2010) Required Warnings for Cigarette Packages and Advertisements. *Federal Register* 75(218), 69523–69565.

United States, Government Accountability Office (2014) Dodd-Frank Regulations: Regulators' Analytical and Coordination Efforts. December. GAO-15-8.

United States, National Institute on Drug Abuse (2012) Drug Facts: Understanding Drug Abuse and Addiction. www.drugabuse.gov/publications/drugfacts/under standing-drug-abuse-addiction.

United States, Office of Management and Budget (2003) *Circular A-4, Regulatory Analysis.* September 17.

(2015) *2015Report to Congress on the Benefits and Costs of Federal Regulations and Unfunded Mandates on State, Local, and Tribal Entities.* Office of Information and Regulatory Affairs.

United States, Social and Behavioral Sciences Team (2016) *Annual Report.* National Science and Technology Council, Executive Office of the President.

United States, Substance Abuse and Mental Health Services Administration (2014) *Results from the 2013 National Survey on Drug Use and Health: Summary of National Findings.* Publication No. SMA 14-4863. Rockville, MD: Department of Health and Human Services.

Varey, Carol and Daniel Kahneman (1992) Experiences Extended Across Time: Evaluation of Moments and Episodes. *Journal of Behavioral Decision Making* 5(3), 169–185.

Vickrey, William (1961) Counterspeculation, Auctions, and Competitive Sealed Tenders. *Journal of Finance* 16(1), 8–37.

Vining, Aidan R. and David L. Weimer (1988) Information Asymmetry Favoring Sellers: A Policy Framework. *Policy Sciences* 21(4), 281–303.

(1992) Welfare Economics as the Foundation for Public Policy: Incomplete and Flawed but Nevertheless Desirable. *Journal of Socio-Economics* 21(1), 25–37.

(2010) An Assessment of Important Issues Concerning the Application of Benefit-Cost Analysis to Social Policy. *Journal of Benefit-Cost Analysis* 1(1), 1–38.

Viscusi, W. Kip (1989) Prospective Reference Theory: Toward and Explanation of the Paradoxes. *Journal of Risk and Uncertainty* 2(3), 235–264.

(1990) Do Smokers Underestimate Risks? *Journal of Political Economy* 98(6), 1253–1269.

(2002) *Smoke-Filled Rooms: A Postmortem on the Tobacco Deal.* Chicago: University of Chicago Press.

(2013) Using Data from the Census of Fatal Occupational Injuries to Estimate the Value of a Statistical Life. *Monthly Labor Review* 136 (October): www .bls.gov/opub/mlr/2013/article/using-data-from-the-census-of-fatal-occupational-injuries-to-estimate-the.htm.

(2015a) The Role of Publication Selection Bias in Estimates of the Value of a Statistical Life. *American Journal of Health Economics* 1(1), 27–52.

(2015b) Reference-Dependence Effects in Benefit Assessment: Beyond the WTA–WTP Dichotomy and WTA–WTP Ratios. *Journal of Benefit-Cost Analysis* 6(1), 187–206.

Viscusi, W. Kip and Joseph E. Aldy (2003) The Value of a Statistical Life: A Critical Review of Market Estimates throughout the World. *Journal of Risk and Uncertainty* 27(1), 5–76.

Viscusi, W. Kip and Ted Gayer (2015) Behavioral Public Choice: The Behavioral Paradox of Government Policy. *Harvard Journal of Law and Public Policy* 38(3), 973–1007.

(2016) Rational Benefit Assessment for an Irrational World: Toward a Behavioral Transfer Test. *Journal of Benefit-Cost Analysis* 7(1), 69–91.

Visschers, Vivianne H. M., Ree M. Meertens, Wim W. F. Passchier, and Nanne N. K. de Vries (2009) Probability Information in Risk Communication: A Review of the Research Literature. *Risk Analysis* 29(2), 267–287.

Volkow, Nora D. and Ting-Kai Li. (2004) Drug Addiction: The Neurobiology of Behaviour Gone Awry. *Nature Reviews Neuroscience* 5(12), 963–970.

von Neumann, John and Oskar Morgenstern (1944) *Theory of Games and Economic Behavior.* Princeton: Princeton University Press.

Vortherms, Sam A. (2014) *Explaining the WTP/WTA Gap: The Issue of Budget Constraint and Unlimited Valuations.* Department of Political Science, University of Wisconsin–Madison: Unpublished Manuscript.

Vossler, Christian A., Maurice Doyon, and Daniel Rondeau (2012) Truth in Consequentiality: Theory and Field Evidence on Discrete Choice Experiments. *American Economic Journal: Microeconomics* 4(4), 145–171.

Vuchinich, Rudy E. and Nick Heather (2003) *Choice, Behavioural Economics and Addiction.* Oxford: Pergamon.

Warner, Mildred E. (2013) Private Finance for Public Goods: Social Impact Bonds. *Journal of Economic Policy Reform* 16(4), 303–319.

Weimer, David L. (1990) An Earmarked Fossil fuels Tax to Save the Rain Forests. *Journal of Policy Analysis and Management* 9(2), 254–259.

(2015) The Thin Reed: Accommodating Weak Evidence for Critical Parameters in Cost-Benefit Analysis. *Risk Analysis* 35(6), 1101–1113.

Weimer, David L. and Aidan R. Vining (2009) *Investing in the Disadvantaged: Assessing the Benefits and Costs of Social Policies.* Washington, DC: Georgetown University Press.

(2011) *Policy Analysis: Concepts and Practice,* 5th edn. Upper Saddle River: Pearson.

Weimer, David L., Aidan R. Vining, and Randall K. Thomas (2009) Cost-Benefit Analysis Involving Addictive Goods: Contingent Valuation to Estimate

Willingness-to-Pay for Smoking Cessation. *Health Economics* 18(2), 181–202.

Weitzman, Martin L. (1998) Why the Far-Distant Future Should Be Discounted at Its Lowest Possible Rate. *Journal of Environmental Economics and Management* 36(3), 201–208.

White, Darcy and Gary Van Landingham (2015) Benefit-Cost Analysis in the States: Status, Impact, and Challenges. *Journal of Benefit-Cost Analysis* 6 (2), 369–399.

Whittington, Dale and Duncan MacRae (1986) The Issue of Standing in Cost-Benefit Analysis. *Journal of Policy Analysis and Management* 5(4), 665–682.

Willig, Robert D. (1976) Consumer's Surplus without Apology. *American Economic Review* 66(4), 589–597.

Wilson, Timothy D. and Daniel T. Gilbert (2003) Affective Forecasting. *Advances in Experimental Social Psychology* 35, 345–411.

Winston, Gordon C. (1980) Addiction and Backsliding: A Theory of Compulsive Consumption. *Journal of Economic Behavior & Organization* 1(4), 295–324.

Wunder, Sven, Stefanie Engel, and Stefano Pagiola (2008) Taking Stock: A Comparative Analysis of Payments for Environmental Services Programs in Developed and Developing Countries. *Ecological Economics* 65(4), 834–852.

Yaari, Menahem E. (1987) The Dual Theory of Choice under Risk. *Econometrica* 55(1), 95–115.

Zerbe, Richard O., Jr. (2001) *Economic Efficiency in Law and Economics*. Northampton: Edward Elgar.

(2004) Should Moral Sentiments Be Incorporated into Benefit-Cost Analysis? An Example of Long-Term Discounting. *Policy Sciences* 37(3–4), 305–318.

Zhang, Anming, Anthony E. Boardman, David Gillen, and I. I. Waters (2004) Towards Estimating the Social and Environmental Costs of Transportation in Canada. *Report for Transport Canada*. Vancouver: Centre for Transportation Studies, University of British Columbia.

Index